brilliant

passing
psychometric
tests

PEARSON

At Pearson, we believe in learning – all kinds of learning for all kinds of people. Whether it's at home, in the classroom or in the workplace, learning is the key to improving our life chances.

That's why we're working with leading authors to bring you the latest thinking and best practices, so you can get better at the things that are important to you. You can learn on the page or on the move, and with content that's always crafted to help you understand quickly and apply what you've learned.

If you want to upgrade your personal skills or accelerate your career, become a more effective leader or more powerful communicator, discover new opportunities or simply find more inspiration, we can help you make progress in your work and life.

Pearson is the world's leading learning company. Our portfolio includes the Financial Times and our education business, Pearson International.

Every day our work helps learning flourish, and wherever learning flourishes, so do people.

To learn more, please visit us at **www.pearson.com/uk**

brilliant

passing
psychometric
tests

Tackling selection tests with confidence

Rachel Mulvey

PEARSON

Harlow, England • London • New York • Boston • San Francisco • Toronto • Sydney • Auckland • Singapore • Hong Kong
Tokyo • Seoul • Taipei • New Delhi • Cape Town • São Paulo • Mexico City • Madrid • Amsterdam • Munich • Paris • Milan

PEARSON EDUCATION LIMITED

Edinburgh Gate
Harlow CM20 2JE
United Kingdom
Tel: +44 (0)1279 623623
Web: www.pearson.com/uk

First published 2015 (print and electronic)

© Pearson Education Limited 2015 (print and electronic)

The right of Rachel Mulvey to be identified as author of this work has been
asserted by her in accordance with the Copyright, Designs and Patents Act 1988.

Pearson Education is not responsible for the content of third-party internet sites.

ISBN: 978-1-292-01651-1 (print)
      978-1-292-01653-5 (PDF)
      978-1-292-01654-2 (ePub)
      978-1-292-01652-8 (eText)

British Library Cataloguing-in-Publication Data
A catalogue record for the print edition is available from the British Library

Library of Congress Cataloging-in-Publication Data
A catalog record for the print edition is available from the Library of Congress

10 9 8 7 6 5 4 3 2 1
19 18 17 16 15

Series cover design by David Carroll & Co
Print edition typeset in Plantin MT Pro by Lumina Datamatics
Print edition printed in Malaysia (CTP-PJB)

To HG & EG

Contents

About the author

Professor Rachel Mulvey is Associate Dean of Psychology at the University of East London, and Associate Fellow at Warwick University. A chartered psychologist, she is an associate fellow of the British Psychological Society and has been awarded a National Teaching Fellowship by the Higher Education Academy. The Transferable Employability Skills Scale (TESS) psychometric she devised for BBCLabUK has been used by over 36,000 young people, and features in Pearson's online course for undergraduates: MyEmployablityLab. With Dr Judith Done, Rachel co-authored *Brilliant Graduate Career Handbook*, now in its 2nd edition.

Author acknowledgements

I am very grateful to all those who helped me sharpen my thinking and clarify what I wanted to get across in this book; as I shared my thinking very readily with friends, family and colleagues, I'm afraid that they really are too numerous to thank by name. My thanks nonetheless. I very much wanted readers to hear from recent graduates who had found their own way through psychometric tests. Devika, Ed, Guy, Hannah, Lyndsey and Rish were very generous in sharing their experience with me and my readers, for which I am most grateful. I'd also like to point out that they are an awesome handful of talent. Three employers were equally generous with their time and insight: Sara Reading who is Head of Early Career Recruitment at the Royal Bank of Scotland, Sim Sekhon who is Director of Legal4Landlords, and Oliver Weedon who is a Business Analyst.

A key message of this book is that practising tests in advance can help to combat nerves, which is a good thing because nerves can prevent you from performing at your best. Another key message is that psychometric tests are serious scientific instruments which have to satisfy demanding design standards if they are to be trusted. So it was important to include test questions in this book, and to have confidence that those tests would be reliable. I was thrilled that Oliver Savill, Director of Assessment Day was so positive when I first approached him about including some of their tests in this book, and am very grateful to have had their permission to do so.

How to use this book

Your brilliant learning

Prepare for the tests which are used by the employer you're applying to

If you are reading this book, it is probably because you are applying for a job and realise you have to get through some psychometric tests as part of the selection process. The five most common types are: verbal reasoning; numerical reasoning; inductive reasoning; situational judgement tests; and personality tests. It is unlikely that you will have to take the entire range of tests, but you are likely to have to go through a couple of different types.

Where employers use psychometric testing as part of their selection process, they often include examples of the kind of test they use somewhere on their website or in their recruitment publications. It makes sense for you to focus on what the employer wants; pick out the relevant sections and concentrate your efforts on them. Check with the employer you are applying to, so as to find out what kind of tests they are using.

> ### brilliant tip
>
> When applying for a vacancy, check out what tests the employer is using and make sure you practise them. Employer websites would normally include a brief rundown of what you can expect in their selection process.

Managing your own learning so you know for sure what you know

Your learning, your way

You set the pace for your learning and you choose what you want to learn about passing psychometric tests. This text will definitely help you and should be a source of support and encouragement. But the only person who decides how much you learn and how well is you. Taking the tests is for your benefit; it identifies what you know and what you still need to work on. Try to see the tests as a measure of distance travelled, helping you to work out how much further you need to go to get through the tests that stand between you and the advertised vacancy.

Brilliant learning

Checking what you have understood is a fundamental step in managing your own learning. You'll be very familiar with this concept from your own education, whether that was at school, college or university either currently, fairly recently or even in the dim and distant past. Managing learning is actually a really important skill once you're in a job too, because it enables you to improve and progress. So taking responsibility for your own learning not only helps you with passing psychometric tests, it also develops a skill which employers are actively seeking in job applicants. 'Brilliant learning' is included at the start of every chapter, so you know what you're getting to grips with.

Brilliant practice

At the end of each section you should check out your learning by taking the relevant test, which is located in Part 3, Brilliant practice. This might be a quick true/false quiz which you can do in five minutes, or a practice reasoning test which might take the best part of an hour. Do it under test conditions, don't allow yourself any distractions, and keep at it until you've worked through to the end.

'I was wildly unprepared for my first test, but, after putting in some research, other than the first initial shock they all began to be similar to one another.'

Ed, BSc Politics, Philosophy and Economics

Brilliant answers

You can then check how well you got on by looking at the worked answers. These explain step by step how the question should be tackled so that you get to the right answer. This gives you another learning opportunity as you can work out how to get it right next time. All the answers to all the tests are located in Part 4, Brilliant answers.

The tests are there to show you what you know for sure; they are there to support you and to reassure you as you learn how to pass psychometric tests.

brilliant dos and don'ts

Do

✔ Choose which sections of this text you need to work through, depending on which tests your preferred employer uses for selection.

✔ Take time to read through the worked answers because this will also help you learn how to improve in that test.

✔ See the tests as milestones along your personal learning journey to check on your progress.

Don't

✘ Be scared of the tests – they are there to reassure and support you.

✘ Skip the tests – they tell you what you've now mastered and where you might need to do a bit more practice.

▶

PART 1

Introduction to psychometric tests

CHAPTER 1

What are psychometric tests?

 **learning**

By the end of this chapter you will understand five different types of tests which are commonly used by employers as part of the selection and recruitment process.

1.1 What are psychometric tests?

Having to take psychometric tests when applying for a job you want can seem a lot to take on, and it is fair to say that where such tests are routinely used for recruitment, it is likely to be part of a selection process which is both thorough and highly competitive. Getting your head round what the tests involve will help you to approach them with a degree of confidence, which should in turn allow you to perform at your best. That is, after all, the ideal outcome both for you as a job applicant and also for the employer: you get a job you really want and they get a new recruit who is well suited to the job they wanted to fill.

What does a psychometric actually do?

Fundamentally, a psychometric (or psychometric test) is a measure of the mind. It might measure ability or aptitude; this is the case where the answer can be deemed right – or wrong. Or it can simply measure – just as a thermometer measures temperature. A psychometric should measure objectively, without bias.

Can I trust a psychometric test?

The simple answer is: yes, you can trust a psychometric test. Just as a thermometer was developed out of scientific work, so psychometrics are developed by psychologists working to exacting scientific principles and constraints. This process will involve close consideration of what questions are included and how they are worded. Everything in the test will be refined, using sophisticated analytical techniques. The design of the test will focus resolutely on the aptitude or ability under scrutiny; a maths test should not be a test of reading ability.

This scientific discipline ensures that the measure is both reliable and valid. That means the measure will produce similar results when used over time and with different groups, and that it will be relevant to its intended purpose and will measure only what it sets out to measure.

Psychometrics are also designed and tested to be objective and it is this quality of treating everyone who completes them in the same way which makes them a valuable part of the selection and recruitment process.

Do psychometrics tell us everything we need to know?
Although we can rely on psychometrics as an objective measure, they can't tell us everything we need to know. That goes both for the applicant and the recruiting employer. Let's use the concrete example of measuring height. If height is measured, we can be confident that we know, for sure, someone is 5'6" tall. That's all we know. But if we know that they are applying to be cabin crew in an airline for which the minimum height is 5'2" and the maximum height is 6'3" then we know that their height fits within those parameters, which means they can be considered as a viable applicant, if only on the height criterion. Of course, we don't know how the person measured feels about being that height, or even if they think themselves quite tall or not tall enough. That's not what was being measured. So psychometrics can't tell us everything we need to know, which is why they are often used alongside other selection tools in a recruitment process.

1.2 Five types of psychometric tests commonly used in selection

There are hundreds of psychometric tests used across the world every day, but what you really need to know about are the handful of measures which are very commonly used in selection, particularly where the selection is relatively non-technical and non-specialist – a graduate management trainee scheme for example. These include ability/aptitude tests for:

1 Verbal reasoning

2 Numerical (also called non-verbal) reasoning

3 Inductive (also called abstract or diagrammatic) reasoning

4 Situational judgement tests (including in-tray exercises) and

5 Personality tests or indicators

Testing reasoning ability in three different ways: verbal, numerical and inductive

It makes sense to look at the first three of these tests as a cluster, because they share a common purpose. Each of them tests how you reason: how you solve a problem by working through it systematically, using logic and reason to get to the right answer. In all of these reasoning tests there is only one correct answer. That may come as no surprise when you think about working with numbers (in the numerical tests) and diagrams (in the abstract or inductive tests) but might seem less likely for the verbal tests. It is nevertheless the case: you have to work out what is the only correct answer you can deduce from reading a piece of written text. It isn't about how well you understand the text (although that does come into it) and it certainly isn't about how well you can express yourself in writing, as that would be measured by a different test altogether. Verbal reasoning, just as much as numerical and inductive reasoning, is about working through a thinking process logically so that you identify a statement which is correct as a conclusion derived from the text you are given.

Reasoning ability doesn't change across employer

The reasoning tests are standard across many different organisations and employment sectors; the same tests tend to be used no matter if you are working in the private sector or the public

brilliant definition

Reasoning tests
There are three different types of reasoning test: verbal (which uses words), non-verbal (which uses numbers), and inductive/abstract/ diagrammatic (which all use diagrams). All of them are designed to test how you work through a problem systematically, using logic and reason to get to the right answer. There is only one right answer in reasoning tests.

sector, in finance or retail or education or health. This makes sense, because it is your ability to reason which is being tested; no matter what capacity or context you'll eventually work in, this demand stays the same.

Testing your judgement of complex or competing demands

The situational judgement test (SJT for short) measures your core competencies by examining how you react to a number of scenarios or imaginary episodes. The kind of competencies would typically be: working in a team, leading and managing people, effective communication, problem-solving, and prioritising tasks. These competencies are transferable across jobs and employers and sectors, so SJTs are used widely.

brilliant definition

Situational judgement tests
Situational judgement tests reproduce the kind of real-life problems you are likely to encounter if you were actually doing the job you are applying for. Often the test is looking for the most effective answer for that particular company in its particular context.

Testing whether your judgement fits with
the organisational values

An SJT is often developed very specifically from the business and/or experience to be found on a day-to-day basis in a particular job. SJTs test how you approach the kind of problem you are likely to encounter in the workplace of the organisation you are applying to, and how well the way you would most likely tackle this problem matches up to how the company would want the problem to be tackled. Some SJTs are designed to probe both for competence and for personality; either way, the test will have been designed to ensure that it looks at exactly what is needed for the job – nothing more, nothing less.

There will be a preferred answer that the test is looking for, but there will also be a close second answer which might be an effective way of tackling the problem you've been presented with, but won't be the answer the company is ideally looking for. Just as much science lies behind SJT questions and answers as in the battery of reasoning tests; this is to ensure that the tests are reliable. The preferred answer will have been rated in the test design phase by a panel of experts who understand the scenarios presented, often because they have had direct experience in that work role or in that employment sector.

 'SJTs are not at all technical. They're a lot about pressures and judgements and team-working and doing the right thing. No prior knowledge is needed and no work experience is needed.'

Sara Reading, Royal Bank of Scotland

You can get a good sense of how the organisation thinks and the skillset and mindset it values by looking at information on its website or in its recruitment brochure. Employers are often explicit about their values and the skills they prize in their employees; this is because they want a good fit between the employee and the job, and they don't want to waste either your time (as an applicant) or their time (as a recruiter) if the fit just isn't there.

brilliant recap

- SJTs test your judgement of typical work scenarios.
- One answer will reflect most closely how the company likes to operate.
- Some SJTs probe for personality type as well as competence.

1.3 In-tray exercise to see how you actually manage competing demands

The in-tray exercise is included here because again it asks you to put yourself in the kind of position you are applying for and tests how you would tackle a typical day's work in that business. The in-tray exercise is very practical. You'll start off as if you were working at that company in the job you are applying for. You'll be presented with a set of tasks and some documents you'll need to work on. Once the test starts you may well receive emails or notifications which make new and competing demands on your time. This is a good way to put you under the kind of pressure you will encounter in the job – and see how you manage.

brilliant tip

Do notice the organisation's values, the skills and attitudes they prize, and keep them in mind when doing SJTs and in-tray exercises.

1.4 Personality tests and indicators

Personal qualities are also very important in a job, so personality tests (sometimes called personality indicators) are used to measure your beliefs, values, motivation, drive and – personality. With personality tests, there isn't really a right or wrong answer; the test is there simply to measure. Being a psychometric, the test does of course give an objective measure against a range of personal qualities, and the strength of those qualities may be important for the job advertised. However, the recruitment process may be looking for the scores in a personality test that fit the job profile of the vacancy they are recruiting to fill. If the job requires a lot of interaction with the general public, a level of extraversion would be sought. If the job requires that care is taken and a certain amount of vigilance then a level of conscientiousness is called for. Taking a personality test can offer fresh insight into what makes you tick, or you may find the test confirms what you have always known about yourself.

 **recap**

> Personality tests look at what makes you tick and give a sense of how you might fit into the job and the company. You don't have to work out the right answer, just be honest about who you are.

Responding to personality tests

There are two slightly different ways in which personality test questions are presented, but in both cases there will be a set of statements. You might be asked to indicate to what extent you think these statements apply to you, putting your answer on a scale running from 'agree strongly' through a neutral position to 'disagree strongly' at the opposite end of the scale. Alternatively, you might be asked to rank your responses, so you will indicate which statements you most agree or most disagree with, as applied to you. The technical difference is that ranking responses is ipsative and rating responses is normative. Normative tests are more common, so you are more likely to be asked to rate yourself along a scale of agreement with a set of statements. There isn't a right answer, so all you have to do is read the question carefully and give your response. You do need to keep your concentration levels up and that can be hard when there are lots of questions, some of which will be asking pretty much the same thing but in slightly different ways. Going by instinct is a good approach; you don't want to over-think your answer because that might distort the picture.

You, just the way you are

You might hear people say that a strategic approach is to work out what kind of personality the employer is looking for and choose the answers that will make you out to be that type. That's really not a good strategy. Firstly, personality tests are carefully designed and you'd need to be very smart indeed to fool the test. Secondly, what would be the point of making up a version of you that might fit with your idea of what the company wants – that just means you'll end up in a job that doesn't really fit with the kind of person you are. What both you and the employer want is an accurate sense of what makes you tick. The real you, not a manufactured identikit or replica; you, just the way you are.

brilliant dos and don'ts

Do

✔ Take tests seriously; they are used to select for the next stage.

✔ Practise reasoning tests so you are confident.

✔ Check on employers' websites for which tests they use.

Don't

✘ Over-think personality tests; just relax and be yourself.

✘ Ignore the advice about practice – just have a go!

1.5 What's it like, doing the different sorts of tests?

Reasoning tests

It is hard to say what it's like to take these tests; the only way you're going to know for sure is by – well, by taking a test. That's why practice tests are included here for you to try out. The reasoning tests (verbal, non-verbal and inductive) tend to be more stressful in that you know you are trying to work out which is the right answer, and you are doing so against the clock. You'll also be using a calculator for the non-verbals and possibly some scrap paper for notes so that's another thing you have to learn to handle. When these tests are taken online there is a countdown timer running down on the screen which can be distracting and unnerving. Practice tests help you get used to both of these pressures.

 'Reasoning tests are no fun, but they're not meant to be. You can prepare, and I would advise it.'

Hannah, BSc Economics and Politics

Situational judgement tests

In situational judgement tests you'll be doing a lot of reading. The challenge here is to think yourself into the situation and to pay attention to what kind of answer you're being asked for. The time pressure might not feel so great but you still need to get through everything; again, practice can help you to pace yourself in reading, thinking and choosing.

Personality tests and indicators

Many people find the personality tests the easiest of all the psychometrics; there's no right answer and there isn't the same kind of time pressure you find in the reasoning tests. Of course, it is possible to feel anxious about personality tests too and to start stressing out about whether the answer you are drawn to is the answer the test is looking for. There is no point going down this path; the tests are designed in such a way as to be rather difficult to second-guess or to manipulate. And even if you were to work out what answer was the one being looked for (and honestly, that is a very difficult thing even for chartered psychologists to do) all you'd achieve by distorting your answers to fit would be to get closer to a job that actually you are temperamentally unsuited for. Far better to work through the questions calmly and answer them honestly. It can feel like there are a lot of questions to get through, and it can feel like some of the questions repeat themselves. If you find yourself tripping up over a question, just take another moment to read it through and go with your instinct; your first answer is probably the best one. Relaxing into the personality test while keeping alert is probably the best approach.

 **brilliant** recap

- Psychometric tests are used to measure ability and aptitude.
- Reasoning tests are commonly used in graduate and other formal training schemes.
- Reasoning tests can be verbal (words) or non-verbal (numbers) or inductive (diagrams) but all of them need you to think logically.
- In situational judgement tests you decide what action you would take in a workplace scenario.
- In-tray exercises simulate a typical work scenario; you are often presented with new tasks and/or information over time.
- Personality tests are all about you; they can enrich your self-knowledge and insight, and help you work out if the job in question is really what you want.

1.6 How do I know what tests an employer uses?

Employers don't make a secret about what tests they use and many of them not only tell you what to expect but make a point of telling you to familiarise yourself with the tests they use by doing some practice tests before you apply for their advertised job. Usually this information can be found in their promotional or recruitment literature (very often you can find this online in the company's website, typically in the Careers or Vacancies or Working For Us section). Once you've identified which tests they use, you can read about each type of test in more detail. There are worked examples of each of the five test types later in this text. You can take a whole test in the practice section of this text (Part 3, Brilliant practice) and find all the answers, along with full explanation of how to get to that answer, in the final section (Part 4, Brilliant answers). There is also a list of websites for your practice; some of these offer online tests under timed conditions.

brilliant dos and don'ts

Do

✔ Check the employer's website for which type of test they use in recruitment.

✔ Read more about each test in this text.

✔ Try the practice tests included in Part 3, Brilliant practice.

Don't

✗ Avoid practice – work through the example questions.

✗ Forget online practice tests will have a built-in timer.

Practice helps performance

Throughout this text, you will be encouraged to practise. This is so you become familiar with what the tests want and how you tackle them. This should give you the confidence to perform authentically when you are taking the test for real. That means you are able to perform as you would if nerves didn't get in the way.

 "The key is practice, practice, practice, practice."

Sara Reading, Royal Bank of Scotland

You don't need to take a practice test immediately after you've read about it, but you do need to take the practice test included in this text at some time. This is so you know for sure what you know, which means that when you come to tackle the tests for real you know what you need to do and you're confident you can do your best.

 practice

Now check what you've learnt about psychometric tests by taking the Chapter 1 true/false quiz in Part 3, Brilliant practice. It should only take 5 minutes.

CHAPTER 2

Why do employers use psychometric tests?

> ⤴ **brilliant** learning
>
> By the end of this chapter you will:
>
> 1 understand why employers use psychometric tests for selection and talent management
>
> 2 know how psychometric tests are used alongside other selection techniques.

2.1 Why do employers use psychometrics in selection and recruitment?

Psychometrics, assessments and measures used by employers include ability and aptitude tests, situational judgement tests and personality indicators. Using these tools may once have been considered a relatively rare method of selecting staff, and you will come across many people working today who did not need to succeed in a psychometric test to get hired. It is certainly true to say that application forms and interviews are a much more common experience for jobseekers. However, within certain sectors and for certain types of employment, the use of psychometrics is well established and, if anything, on the increase. This definitely applies to both modern apprenticeships and graduate trainee schemes. Such schemes typically would include: training for management (e.g. in supermarkets and retail stores, the Civil Service and the National Health Service), training for other specialist roles (e.g. economist or analyst) and training for chartership in a profession (e.g. accountant or civil engineer). In fact, if you are applying for these kinds of jobs, you may feel that every employer you come across is using psychometrics. And you may well ask yourself why that is. There are a number of answers, which ultimately boil down to the employer's concern to ensure that they recruit the best person for the job.

People who do well in psychometrics tend to perform well in their job

Broadly speaking, employers use psychometrics as part of their selection processes to ensure that they employ the best person for the job on offer. Research shows the proven link between how someone performs in a psychometric test and how they perform once actually in the job. So good performance by a job applicant in the psychometric gives the employer confidence about good performance on the job. This matters because paying wages is very often the biggest cost companies have to meet, month after month. If an employer can be confident that the right person is in place to do the job that the organisation needs doing for its commercial success, that's a good place to be.

'If they are good in the tests they are going to be good at what they do. With the personality style question-naires, how high they score on pragmatist and extra-vert relates to how well they do their job.'

Sim Sekhon, Managing Director, Legal4Landlords

People who do well in psychometrics tend to enjoy their job

The economic reason is compelling, but another part of the answer is that, generally speaking, people who are happy and confident in their work tend to work better. However, the key to understanding why employers are using psychometrics is to stop and think about the kind of jobs we are talking about here. No matter what the job title, no matter if the level is gradu-ate or higher level apprenticeships, these kinds of jobs make a very explicit offer of systematic training. There is no doubt that the employee will invest heavily in terms of time and effort – just ask any graduate management trainee working full time and taking professional postgraduate exams in their first year. The employer is investing heavily too, by offering a structured high-level training. Using psychometrics as part of the selection process justifiably increases the probability of ensuring there is a good fit between employee and employment for the benefit of all concerned – including customers and all other stakeholders.

 'Before having done any of these tests, I was nervous and cynical – I doubted that the employer could really ascertain any real information about my capacity from such a limited overview. However after a few practices I quickly realised that most employers tend to use the same questions or very similar – highlighting that such a process is simply looking for a "minimum standard" of candidate.'

Devika, BSc Politics, Philosophy and Economics

Psychometrics can be used to develop staff once they are in the job

The main focus of this text is how best to prepare yourself for psychometric tests so as to get a job. That's why the emphasis in this chapter is how employers use psychometrics to recruit people – that is, to take them on and place them in a job. Given the link between testing and performance, employers can also use psychometrics to develop their people in the course of their employment. There is a good example of this approach to talent management in a legal services company (Legal4Landlords) where, over and above their weekly targets, every employee has a formal meeting once a year in which their performance is reviewed, overall targets are set for the coming year and, crucially, opportunities for career development can be discussed. Psychometrics come into play here and can be used to see how far someone has developed in a role and what possible roles they could play in a team in the future.

'We use the personality style questionnaire too every year with appraisals.'

Sim Sekhon, Managing Director, Legal4Landlords

2.2 Psychometrics are a way of measuring objectively

Psychometrics offer an objective measure of competence or aptitude. If you've studied psychology, you'll know in some detail exactly how much scientific rigour goes into the construction and publication of a psychometric test. As a job applicant faced with tackling psychometric tests, you don't need to know the inner workings of these tests. It is, however, important that you understand that psychometrics are not taken lightly; they are treated as seriously as any other measure which is used to make comparisons and to arrive at judgements. In this case, the judgement of whether to offer a job – or not. As a measure, or measuring instrument, a published psychometric must satisfy stringent requirements about validity and reliability. Above all, the measure should be objective, so that it applies equally to everyone measured, without the risk of bias or favour which can, even unwittingly, creep into other more subjective means of selection.

'If you're good at them it distinguishes you from the rest of the applicants. It gives employers something solid that they can judge your abilities on, rather than the sometimes quite broad application questions.'

Guy, BSc Politics, Philosophy and Economics

Are they really objective or do they discriminate against minority populations?

You may have concerns that if you don't fit into a majority population, a psychometric might in some way discriminate against you. Rest assured that any bias should be tested out of a psychometric before it is used on the diverse populations of today. This is part of the scientific rigour behind the development of an assessment; if there were any bias it would make the test unreliable and no test producer wants that.

'We use psychologists to validate tests to make sure there's no bias.'

Sara Reading, Royal Bank of Scotland

Employers want to ensure they recruit on talent not on bias

Apart from genuine concern about operating fairly (by avoiding any discrimination against a particular group), no employer wants to use a test that might rule out good people. They are far more concerned about getting talented people to work for them and welcome the fact that tests focus purely on performance in a given role. Testing also works well in focussing on what you are capable of right here and now.

'I pretty much insist, from what I've found works in business, on using psychometrics to sort the wheat from the chaff. Using tests means there was no bias; we just wanted the right people for that particular job.'

Oliver Wheedon, Business Analyst

2.3 How can I take the test if I have special needs or some kind of disability?

If you do have any special needs, you should bring these to the attention of the employer well in advance of the testing, to allow them to make the reasonable adjustments which the law requires. The adjustments would of course vary depending on the particular need you have. This could include assistive software such as voice recognition. Extra time, either for taking the test itself or more likely to allow for more breaks in between sections of the test, might also be permissible. The test or measure itself will not be amended or adapted, because doing that might make the outcome unfair on other applicants. The necessary adjustments are there to ensure that you do not, as a direct result of your disability, suffer any unfair disadvantage in taking the test.

brilliant tip

If you have any kind of special need, learning need or disability, contact the employer well in advance of the test date or cut-off date to discuss this. Reasonable adjustments might be possible, but these will probably need to be agreed well in advance, so contact them as soon as you can.

2.4 Psychometrics as part of selection for both employer and jobseeker

It is clear that employers use psychometric testing as an objective and reliable way of measuring applicants against the demands of a particular job or role within an organisation. Normally, doing well in the appropriate test indicates you are likely to do well in that job and, normally, doing well in a job tends to give a greater sense of satisfaction and enjoyment to the worker. So we can see why employers would use tests to select applicants.

'A big thing about the test is self-selection, helping people decide. We might not be as aggressive an environment as they want to work in. Or they might think it's too fluffy. Or it might totally resonate with them and they might think it's absolutely right for them.'

Sara Reading, Royal Bank of Scotland

Using psychometrics to check your career thinking

But this process of selection works equally well for the job-seeker. So you yourself can use the tests to check whether you are heading in the right career direction. You can even put your test results to one side and look carefully at what you've made of going through the testing process to see if that tells you anything about your career journey. You might come to realise that, having looked more closely at a particular career direction, it doesn't feel right. This can be disappointing and confusing, but it is better to make sense of your career thinking while there's still time to change direction.

 **brilliant** tip

Psychometric testing can help you as a jobseeker work out what role would suit you best. Even working out what wouldn't suit you helps you move forward in your career direction.

2.5 Psychometrics are only part of selection and recruitment

There can be no doubt that these tests are important; with some employers, if you don't hit the benchmark in the online tests, you can't even get as far as submitting an application form. The tests are the gateway into the selection process and if you don't succeed you can't proceed in that recruitment round. Don't be totally disheartened by this; you might be able to try again the following year. The Civil Service is really clear that many of their successful Fast Stream candidates have gone through on their second attempt.

Assuming that you do get through the psychometrics, the employer will inevitably be using further, additional selection techniques. Take the Royal Bank of Scotland as an example. If

brilliant tip

Even if you don't do brilliantly at one of the tests, your overall performance might get you through. Even if you don't succeed the first
time you go through a selection process, some employers allow you
to apply a second time.

you pass the situational judgement test within the online application, you proceed to online logical and numerical reasoning
tests. If you meet the benchmark in these, you will then have
a telephone interview. If you get through the interview, you're
then invited to an assessment centre where you'll go through a
range of assessments. Although you do have to make the benchmark in everything you're assessed on, you don't have to be outstanding at all of them. The selection process puts all of your
scores together and makes a judgement based on your performance in the round.

brilliant practice

Now check what you've learnt about how employers use psychometric tests
by taking the Chapter 2 true/false quiz in Part 3, Brilliant practice. It should
only take 5 minutes.

brilliant recap

- Psychometrics offer a standardised measure of a candidate's
  aptitude and/or ability to do a particular job or role.
- Psychometrics can give a good indication that an individual is
  likely to perform well and/or enjoy doing that job or role.

▶

- There is a lot of scientific rigour behind a reliable psychometric.

- Employers use psychometrics as part of their recruitment and selection process, alongside other methods such as application form and interview.

- Employers can also use psychometrics to support staff development and for talent management.

CHAPTER 3

What to expect and how to prepare for tests

brilliant learning

By the end of this chapter you will:

1 understand how preparing for tests can help you

2 be able to adopt a mindset which minimises nerves and maximises your performance.

3.1 Why bother preparing for psychometric tests?

The main argument for you investing time and effort before even taking psychometric tests is that preparation gives you the best possible chance to show what you can do. These tests are developed rigorously so as to ensure that if it's numerical reasoning that is being tested, that is what the test is designed to do. If an employer wants to gauge how well you perform under pressure then a test will be designed which is fit for that purpose. By getting to understand what these tests are about (and going so far as to practise before you take the test for real) you will be able to handle any nerves to ensure you perform to the best of your ability.

'If someone's got the ability and nerves get in the way, that's not helping them and it's certainly not helping us.'

Sara Reading, Royal Bank of Scotland

Once you are prepared, you can be sure that all your energy and focus goes into solving the problem which is in front of you, rather than using up all your energy working out how on earth you are going to tackle the next question.

'Practice is the key, especially for the reasoning tests. I've found such tests often more influenced by being confident and calm under pressure rather than the actual difficulty. So the key would be to not let the test faze you – and prepare well.'

Devika, BSc Philosophy, Politics and Economics

3.2 Is it cheating to look at the tests before you do them?

This question comes up every so often when psychometric tests are discussed; job applicants question whether they should really be looking at examples and fellow psychologists have even asked me if it is entirely ethical to encourage job applicants to familiarise themselves with the tests and formats. Interestingly, this question is never asked in relation to preparing for exams and assessments; quite the opposite in fact, as in that case students are expected to revise and practise on past papers.

The issue is that psychometric tests, when used as part of a recruitment and/or selection process, are looking for differences between one applicant and another. The British Psychological Society (BPS, 2012) is very clear that while difference is acceptable, *unfair* difference is not acceptable – because that would be bias. Both the employers and successful job hunters quoted in this text give a consistent message: becoming familiar with the test formats and demystifying the test process allows candidates to build confidence and thereby present their authentic self in the application process.

'Practice and preparation allow you to get over your nerves and perform to the best of your ability.'

Sara Reading, Royal Bank of Scotland

Applicants should know to practise psychometrics before taking tests for real.

Many applicants will have taken the opportunity to familiarise themselves with the layout and format of reasoning tests before they take them for real as part of a job application process. If other applicants have had the same opportunities but haven't made the effort, that is of course their choice. But if an applicant doesn't know anything about these tests, and doesn't have the opportunity to practise, that makes for unfairness, which this text aims to counterbalance. Understanding more about psychometrics (why they are used and what they look like) will demystify testing for you and allay the natural fear which is felt when you face something unknown. Learning how to tackle the questions will build your confidence, as will having useful techniques and strategies at your fingertips. All in all, this will support you in a test situation so that you can perform authentically, to the best of your natural ability.

'I would definitely advise preparing for tests. The more familiar one is with the format, the more accurately one shows one's ability to a potential employer.'

Devika, BSc Philosophy, Politics and Economics

Employers actively encourage applicants to practise their tests beforehand

Many of the employers who use psychometrics as part of their recruitment and selection process explicitly advise applicants to familiarise themselves with the tests before they take them for real. Some even offer online practice tests on their own websites. These online tests have a built-in timer, so you get a feel for what it is like taking a test under test conditions. Others encourage you to go online to try the tests for yourself. A list of relevant websites is included at the end of this text.

brilliant tip

Familiarise yourself with tests by working through the examples and practice questions included in this text.

Getting familiar with testing is so important that Part 3 of this book is devoted to tests for you to practise where and when it suits you. In Part 4 you'll find all the answers, along with step by step explanations of how to get to the right answer. There is quite a lot you can do to minimise nerves and thus maximise your performance by thinking through what taking a psychometric test involves. This includes: at what point are you likely to come across them in your career; whether you take them online or on paper; whether online is in your home or somewhere else, and what you can do before, during and after a test. Taking control of what is in your grasp should help you to feel more confident about the challenges of the test itself.

brilliant tip

Practising helps a psychometric measure your true ability, not how well you cope with unexpected pressure.

3.3 When are you likely to take a psychometric test?

Many employers use psychometric tests as an integral part of their selection process, alongside application forms, interviews and assessment centres – which can include all of the above plus some form of group activity. This approach to recruitment is particularly common where the job on offer includes structured training over a number of years such as an apprenticeship or a graduate trainee role.

Psychometric testing at the start of the selection process

Where an employer is offering a job with structured training, it is likely that they are recruiting to a relatively large number of posts – hundreds of jobs in some cases. These are attractive job offers and therefore attract a high number of applicants – easily numbering thousands for some employers. Take the Civil Service Fast Stream for example: in just one year there were 23,200 applications submitted for between 750 and 800 jobs. That works out to about 30 applicants for each job on offer. Employers use psychometrics so they recruit people who are well suited to the job and are likely to do the job well. But they also use psychometrics as a way of filtering out applicants, which means that unless you achieve a threshold score on the tests, your application won't even be considered and you will be eliminated from that recruitment round. So it is important that you take initial psychometrics seriously because you'll need to get over this initial hurdle.

 'I think taking mock tests can really help; you get used to the nature of the questions and inevitably become better at answering them. Doing practice tests can give you a few more marks which helps in getting over the threshold that allows your application even to be considered.'

Guy, BSc Politics, Philosophy and Economics

Psychometric testing somewhere along the selection process

Psychometrics don't tell us everything we need to know – inevitably, given that they are designed solely to appraise one particular aspect of how your mind works. So the recruitment process often combines tests with other selection methods including: application form, CV, interview and group task. You might find you have to take a psychometric test somewhere along the selection process, typically where you have succeeded in your submitted application and are then invited to take tests either online or in person.

If an employer invites you to an assessment centre, you can expect to spend at least a couple of hours and more often than not an entire day there, going through several of these selection activities, alongside other hopefuls applying for the same job.

Even if you have taken tests online before you are invited to meet up with the employer (either for an interview or at an assessment centre), you might find that you have to take some tests again at the employer's premises or another venue. This is specifically designed to check whether you can perform consistently in tests. It also shows up if it wasn't you who took the initial test online.

brilliant tip

Don't even consider getting someone else to take online tests for you or to do the online test with you. At best you'll end up in a job for which you are simply not suited. At worst you will be found out as unreliable and untrustworthy. Neither outcome is worth risking.

Psychometric testing sometime during your employment

Psychometrics are such a useful way of measuring ability and personality that many employers use them with their workers throughout their employment. They are used right across the board in this way, just as much for very senior positions as for entry-level jobs. Don't be surprised if this happens to you – it is certainly nothing to be worried about. See it as an objective measure of all that you have learned since the last time you took them.

'Nobody likes psychometric tests. They are hideously unpopular. They are the least popular thing in the entire process.'

Sara Reading, Royal Bank of Scotland

3.4 Online or on paper – how tests are administered

Paper-based tests

Not that long ago, psychometric tests were invariably done on paper. Typically you would be invited to attend a session either at the employer's premises or perhaps at some other neutral location (e.g. a dedicated test centre) where the tests would be administered by someone competent to do so. This set-up would feel rather familiar to anyone who has taken an exam: desks laid out and spaced apart in rows, someone at the front of the room or the hall conducting everything. It would not be unusual to see lots of candidates in silence, each working their way through a question booklet, marking answers in pencil on the paper provided.

Online tests

Nowadays it is much, much more likely that you will do a test online. You will either be invited to take the test at a specified location – typically this would be at the employer's premises or possibly some other location, perhaps a purpose-built centre. You would then be given access to a computer set up for you to use for the test. Alternatively, you will be expected to go online to take the test and it will be up to you to arrange access to a computer yourself. As this is the more common approach, let's start here.

3.5 Preparing to take a test online

Managing the test environment at home

If you are taking the test at home, then you can do quite a lot to control the test environment. Because online tests are timed, you really don't want to be disturbed once you've started and the clock is counting down. Log out of anything that might distract you (Facebook, for example) and turn your phone off. Let people who live with you know that you really can't be disturbed by either telling them in advance or putting a notice up somewhere – on a door maybe.

'There is the added pressure of thinking your laptop might crash, someone might ring the doorbell, you might spill your drink on your keyboard etc., but the only thing to do is to mitigate against that as far as you can. Then just get your head down and hope for the best.'

Hannah, BSc Economics and Politics

Choosing when to take the online test
One massive advantage of taking a test online is that you get to decide when you do it. Nobody knows better than you what time of day suits you best; so if you are a night owl you can take it when everyone else is asleep. If you are a morning person, you can take it at daybreak if you want, when (you guessed it) everyone else is asleep. Don't take it at a busy time of day when there is always a lot going on; you don't want to be disturbed and you don't want to be distracted. This is about you doing your very best in the tests, which makes you number one priority.

brilliant tip

Treat an online test that you take at home just like you would treat an exam. Prepare for it carefully, and get into your performance zone before you log on.

Ensuring your computer is up to the task
The first thing you'll need to do is to secure access to a reliable computer. You may have your own PC or laptop already. If not,

you'll need to borrow one, or you might need to book one in a public or university library. You'll need to ensure that the computer is up to the task; this means checking that you are reading in full-screen setting and that the resolution is set to the levels specified by the test. These requirements can be found in the test provider's guide. You might have to install a free plug-in – for example the Civil Service Fast Stream online tests use Microsoft Silverlight. All of these specifications will be laid out in advance; you just need to ensure you give yourself enough time to get everything in place before you log on and take the test in real time.

Ensuring you've got everything you need at hand

Whether you take the test online or at a venue, it is essential to have everything you need with you. This could include your own calculator, your own rough paper and something to write with. Check the batteries in your calculator and that your pens work. You'll need to check what you are expected or indeed allowed to take into a test venue – and you'd need to do that beforehand. Of course, if you wear glasses or have a hearing aid or use a back cushion or anything else that helps you do what you need to do, make sure you've got that to hand.

Ensuring you are comfortable

Given that online tests are nearly always timed, once you start that clock you don't want anything to get in the way of you using every second you've got. So make sure you've had a comfort break before you start, and that you've had something to eat so you don't get distracted by hunger pangs! Make sure you are comfortable; don't do the test with your laptop on your knee but sit at a table, ensuring you've got enough space to do rough calculations on paper.

Managing a neutral test environment

If you need to do a test online but don't have access to a reliable computer at home, you will need to arrange access to a computer at a neutral environment. This could be at your college or university, perhaps in a library or a computer cluster. Public libraries also offer computer access and these kinds of venues should be relatively quiet and comfortable. Book yourself in for a specific time; you really don't want to turn up and find there is nothing available for you.

brilliant tip

If you don't have a reliable computer at home, book one in advance at a public or university library.

Check a booked computer is compatible with the test requirements
Just as you would at home, you'll need to check that the computer you have booked has the technical capacity needed for the tests; this is normally specified on the employer or test provider guide to applicants, so it is just a question of checking it out when you book your computer slot. Gather up everything you need to hand and take it with you. Make sure you're comfortable (comfort break and/or snack beforehand) and off you go.

brilliant dos and don'ts

Do

✔ Ensure the computer you use meets test requirements.

✔ Close down and log out of anything that might distract you.

✔ Take the test at your best time of day.

✔ Practise before you take the test for real.

✔ Ensure you've got calculator/spectacles to hand.

✔ Prepare for an online test just as you would for an exam.

Don't

✗ Start the test when you are hungry or tired.

✗ Get someone else to help or take the test for you.

Managing the external test environment – employer premises or test centre

If the test takes place somewhere specified by the employer, they will ensure interruptions are at a minimum. Check if you can take your own calculator and/or rough paper, and make sure you've got pens and pencils – again, treat it like an exam.

Carefully check the time, date and address on your invitation. If at all possible, try to visit the venue before the test itself, so you have a keen sense of how long that journey takes. Then add some extra time on the day, just to give you some peace of mind when the unforeseeable happens: a traffic jam, a snapped heel, some train delay. If you then find you have arrived at the test venue way too early, think about having a cup of tea or coffee or just walking around the block to clear your head ready for the test.

Sitting the test away from home

If the assessment centre is some distance away then you might even have to stay overnight. Again, do what you can in advance to get everything ready for the big day. The key thing is to allow plenty of time, so when the unforeseen problem happens, you're not thrown off-balance. You can use online maps and journey planners to check venues, train times, transport connections, walking routes and times. Maximise your use of anything that helps you to arrive for your test in the best possible frame of mind to perform well.

3.6 Managing during the test

Make sure you understand what you're being asked to do

Every test comes with its own set of instructions and once you've done a few practice tests these will become very familiar. You still need to make sure you have read and understood the instructions, so give this your attention. These instructions are carefully written, often in quite formal language. They are there to ensure that everyone understands what they need to do to answer the questions; that's all part of psychometrics being constructed rigorously so as to be fair.

In a non-verbal test make sure you know what unit is being asked for (tens, hundreds, thousands, millions) or whether it is a percentage or a ratio you are looking for. In an inductive reasoning test, are you predicting the next in a sequence or which diagram would come earlier in a sequence? In a situational judgement test, do they want to know what you are most likely to do, or what you think would be the most effective course of action? In a personality test, are you being asked to indicate to what extent the statement applies to you, or to rank statements from 'most' to 'least' applying to you. These are crucial differences. The instruction is there in front of you – make sure you read it.

 **brilliant** tip

No test is trying to catch you out – there will be clear instructions; just read them carefully and follow them to the letter.

How to use your time well

There is a strict time limit on most of the reasoning tests; this is most obvious online where the timer countdown kicks off as soon as you start the test. Try to see this as a helpful tool to manage your time well. You've done exams within time limits, and you should have practised your tests within time limits too.

'If they're unprepared and they don't know what to expect, even just the clock ticking down can throw them for six. They'll get in a panic and fail the tests. By the time they've done their third application they'll know what to expect; they're prepared and they'll sail through it.'

Sara Reading, Royal Bank of Scotland

Remember the tips and tools you've learnt for each kind of test and use those strategies to keep moving on through the test. If you come across a question which really stumps you, don't waste time puzzling it out – move on to the next one. You might have time to come back to it, and you might be more in the swing of things so coming back makes it easier.

 'The time pressure of the test is the biggest distraction, but after a few attempts you get used to the time limit and disciplined about allocating time.'

Guy, BSc Politics, Philosophy and Economics

Dealing with feelings of panic

Accept that, in many of the tests, you are not expected to tackle every single question; it is ok to let a few pass by. If you start panicking about not doing well while you are doing the test you have to tell yourself very firmly that you are doing your best and that's all you can reasonably expect of yourself. It is a test and so of course you will feel tested; nothing wrong in that. Use that nervous energy to pull in everything you've practised and go for it.

 **tip**

Breathe out, drop your shoulders. Know that you've done your preparation and therefore you are ready. Focus on the question in front of you, and try to see the whole thing as a learning experience.

3.7 What you can usefully do after you've done a test

The first thing you can usefully do after you've done a test is to rest and relax for a little while. You may find you are more tired that you'd expected; this isn't surprising because you've been concentrating hard and trying to perform at your best.

brilliant tip

Quickly run through the test you've done just to focus on what kind of questions caused you problems. Revise that question type to help you in your next test or in the next phase of the selection process.

There isn't anything you can do about the answers you have given on the test, but you can reflect on the test as a learning experience. This is particularly useful if you are applying for a few different jobs, all of which tend to use psychometrics as part of the selection process.

brilliant practice

Now check what you've learnt about what to expect and how to prepare by taking the completely unscientific personality type indicator (test for Chapter 3) in Part 3, Brilliant practice.

brilliant dos and don'ts

Do
- ✔ Try the practice tests included in this text.
- ✔ Try some practice online tests which have the timer running.
- ✔ Check your PC is ok for online tests.
- ✔ Use a tricky test to pinpoint what you need to revise for next time.
- ✔ Check travel if you are doing tests at a venue.
- ✔ Request reasonable adjustments (for particular needs) well in advance of the test date.

Don't

X   Allow yourself to be distracted – that means no Facebook, no phone.

X   Fret about a difficult question – move on to the next one.

X   Cheat: you will get found out eventually.

X   Agonise about your performance once the test is over.

CHAPTER 4

What if I don't get through?

By the end of this chapter you will know how to use your experience of psychometric tests for personal and professional development.

4.1 What happens if I don't get through?

All the other chapters in this text lead up to the moment of taking a psychometric test as part of a selection process for a job. This is the only chapter which addresses what happens after the test; indeed it tackles the delicate issue of what you can do if you don't get through. Everyone deals with this situation in their own way, from laughing it off, or berating the employer for poor judgement, or sinking into gloom as their self-confidence takes a blow. Once your initial reaction has worn off, you can learn from your experience so as to develop both personally and professionally. This chapter, and its related tests, will show you how.

Not everyone gets through

The brutal truth is that in many cases where psychometric tests are used as part of the selection process, there are many more applicants than there are jobs on offer. This is particularly true of graduate management trainee schemes, where there can be 30 or even 80 or more applicants for each available job. Clearly, not everyone who applies can be successful, so if you don't get through, at least you know that you won't be the only one.

Getting through next time

Many of these competitive schemes run annually, so if you don't get through the first time, you may have the chance to apply the following year. If you go down this route it is really important that you make the most of what you've learnt first time round by using the approaches given here.

 recap

- Not everyone gets through first time.
- You might be able to apply again next time round.
- It's important to learn from your experience so you develop personally and professionally.

4.2 Getting feedback

Feedback from employers

Some employers routinely handle thousands of applications; the NHS scheme attracted over 12,000 and the Civil Service Fast Stream over 23,000 applicants in one year's round. Dealing with applications on this scale means that they do not routinely give individual feedback to unsuccessful applicants. Devika found this frustrating. She also identified that getting insight can help you improve and develop.

 'The thing which frustrates me is the lack of feedback. It seems employers give candidates such tests to make sure they pass a minimum, but not to help them improve or develop from them. I would have appreciated some sort of feedback or insight into what my answers really meant.'

Devika, BSc Philosophy, Politics and Economics

However, some employers routinely do give feedback, perhaps using the test results within the interview process. Both employer and candidate can find this of benefit, as these quotes illustrate:

 'Feedback was given and the test results were a strong contributing factor to me being successful in being appointed.'

Lyndsey, BSc Applied Zoology

'Selection starts with their cv, then longlisted applicants are invited for tests and interview. We give them their results straight away – there's nothing that isn't shared with them.'

Sim Sekhon, Managing Director, Legal4Landlords

Although it is not guaranteed that you will get feedback, you can always go back and ask the employer. If you do approach an employer with this request, be clear in your own head that you are not arguing about the outcome of the process; you accept that you have not been successful on this occasion but want to learn all you can from the experience. Frame your request in this way and be polite and be gracious if you don't get the answer you are hoping for. Remember that feedback can take different forms: it might be your test scores or individual feedback on how you did or more general feedback on all the applicants in that round.

Feedback from practice

Even where there is no feedback forthcoming from employers, there are other sources of feedback. If you've been doing the tests included in this text you will have a sense of how you've performed. Taking example and practice tests online helps you establish your baseline, which means you can then keep track of your progress. You will get a good sense of how you learn to handle the real-time countdown and you can also get feedback on how many correct answers you got and even how your score compares with norm populations. Taking a psychometric test online normally leads to some kind of personal profile – valuable insight into what makes you tick which can either confirm your career plans or give you pause to reflect and maybe refine your career thinking. A selection of online sites is included in this text (see 'Online practice').

Here's some feedback for you

The very fact that you are reading this text means that you are actively engaged in your professional development, and that is something employers definitely want. If you've already worked your way through a chapter and its associated test **(in Part 3, Brilliant practice)** then you have demonstrated that you take responsibility for your own learning, which is something employers rate very highly. So take this as positive feedback: your commitment to your professional development is impressive. The next section shows you how to take that learning to another level.

 **recap**

- Some employers do give feedback, some don't.
- It's always worth asking for feedback. Be clear when making the request that you simply want to learn from your experience and that you're not disputing the selection outcome.
- You can get feedback from doing practice tests both in this book and online.
- Psychometric profiles can enhance your self-knowledge and enrich your self-insight.
- You might need to refine or rethink your career in the light of feedback.
- Getting feedback, and acting on it, shows you are committed to personal and professional development.

4.3 Your learning and your career: doing it your way

Your learning

Looking back over your recent experiences of psychometrics can really help you understand about your own learning, and also about the unique way in which you think – and manage your career. Thinking about what you have learnt and how you have learnt it is a useful skill to develop because it will support you throughout your life both in the personal and the professional domains. Setting out, deliberately, to learn from your experience is reflective learning and reflective learning is helpful because it both speeds up and deepens the learning process.

There is an added bonus in reflective learning; it is a skill that employers rate highly, because it shows that someone is willing to adapt and grow.

 **brilliant** definition

Reflective learning
Reflective learning is when you intentionally learn from your experience.

Reflective learning

Reflective learning comes about when there is an explicit intention to learn from a specific experience. It is purposeful learning in that you have to make an active commitment to engage in this learning process. It is very much a process rather than a one-off event and, ideally, reflective learning should be a lifelong process. That's not to suggest it has to be something that you do every day, but that it is an approach you can use to learn from what you are experiencing in both the personal and the professional aspects of your life. It is personal, in that reflective learning can only be about your unique reactions to what you experience, and what those reactions mean to you. Finally, it is entirely private; what you share or disclose rests with you.

How to get started with reflective learning
Reflective learning is usually presented as a cycle or iterative process; starting with going back to a particular experience,

then thinking through your experience in order to formulate an action or approach that you commit to enacting at some point in the future.

brilliant tip

Pay attention to positive feelings when you are reflecting on your experience; they can help you to locate what worked and why, so you can draw on that again in the future.

Start by choosing a specific incident, then really focus on you in that situation by working through questions such as: *How did you feel? What was going through your mind? How did you react? What did you do? What were your feelings after the action was completed?* Zoom in on you, in your world, as you experienced this event. There can be a skewed focus on negative emotions which can hang around longer and loom larger in your memory. Remember that positive feelings are just as important, and paying attention to what went well helps to isolate what works.

Next, consider whether you would you do anything differently if you found yourself in a similar situation in the future. Would you change your actions? Your behaviour? Your reactions? The way you felt? If everything went well and there is nothing you would change, that's ok; just remember what it was that worked for you so you can draw on that again in the future.

Then you identify what exactly you would do differently and commit to this change in future action.

Finally, you would check again in due course to see whether you actually did implement the new, desired action which came out of your reflection. Which is what brings the whole process full circle.

 recap

- Reflective learning focuses on a specific experience.
- Notice what went well and what went badly – feelings can give you important clues in this.
- Identify what exactly you would do differently.
- Commit to enacting that change in future action.

Your career

If you are looking into psychometrics as part of the process of applying for jobs, you might like to focus some of your attention on how you are managing your career. This might be simply a question of planning your next steps, or making sense of how you are approaching and managing your career. Of course, you may already have done quite a lot of focusing and planning; however, with the feedback you've collected from your experience of psychometric tests, you might need to refocus and maybe rethink your career plans.

 practice

Now check how to use your experience of psychometric tests for personal and professional development by doing the tasks set for Chapter 4 in Part 3, Brilliant practice.

CHAPTER 5

In case of emergency, read here

5.1 It's not too late

If you've turned to this chapter first, it's probably because you are getting desperate. Maybe you have to do some psychometric tests, the deadline is fast approaching and you don't feel as well prepared as you would like. The good news is that, even at this late stage, there are things you can do and tactics you can use.

5.2 What psychometric test are you taking?

Work out which test you're taking

Somewhere on the employer's website, or in their promotional literature, there should be some indication of what tests they use in their selection process. There are five main types:

1 Verbal reasoning

2 Non-verbal or numerical reasoning

3 Inductive, abstract or diagrammatic reasoning

4 Situational judgement tests

5 Personality tests or indicators

Once you know which kind of test you're up against, have a look at the following quick guides, along with the tips and techniques you can use to tackle them.

5.3 What does a verbal reasoning test look like?

What can you expect from a verbal reasoning test? Typically you will be presented first with a piece of text. It won't necessarily be a long piece, maybe only a paragraph or two. What then follows is a set of statements. Your task is to decide for each statement, whether that statement is: (a) True (b) False or (c) Cannot say. Be careful about answer option (c); it doesn't mean the same as 'I don't know'. You choose 'Cannot say' when there is nothing exact in the text that leads you to the conclusion either that the statement is true or that it is false.

How to tackle a verbal reasoning test

Although you will, of course, need to understand the paragraph, a verbal reasoning test is not simply checking your English comprehension. It is testing how you use reason to puzzle out the correct solution to a problem. Part of that testing (of how well you reason) is to see if you make assumptions; that is, whether you bring into your reasoning something which isn't actually there in the text.

brilliant tips

- Read the text first for overview, then re-read it for each statement you have to decide on.
- Focus on one question at a time; justify that one then start afresh on the next.
- If the answer jumps out at you, take a moment to double check your reasoning is sound.
- 'Cannot say' has to be justified in the same way as 'true' or 'false'.
- The answer will be there in the text: look closely to locate it.
- If you are really stuck on a question, move on to the next.

Verbal reasoning tests are timed, so you have to find a balance between speed and accuracy. It can be disconcerting to see the timer ticking down (fast) so use these strategies to minimise your stress and maximise your performance.

brilliant dos and don'ts

Do

✔ Read the text carefully.
✔ Read each question carefully.
✔ Identify what it is in the text that you have used as the justification for your answer.

▶

Don't

✗ Jump to conclusions.

✗ Bring in any prior knowledge; stick to the text given.

✗ Choose 'cannot say' as a default answer.

5.4 What does a non-verbal/numerical reasoning test look like?

Numerical reasoning tests follow a pretty standard format; there will be a chunk of numerical data which could be presented as a graph, or in a table, or combination of the two. You will then have to use the data to answer a question, or series of questions, by choosing the correct answer in a multiple choice answer format. Once you've understood what the question is asking you to calculate, the arithmetic you'll need to do is really not complex. If you haven't handled percentages, fractions and ratios for a while, it's worth refreshing your memory. Just one hour on a GCSE-level website might make all the difference. Try: **www. bbc.co.uk/education/subjects/z6pfb9q.**

brilliant tips

● You will need to handle percentages, fractions, ratios and differing units.

● You will need to spot increases as opposed to decreases.

● You need to be able to make sense of graphs, tables, bar and pie charts.

● Test formats can vary but all test the same numerical reasoning skills, so if you can do one, you can do them all.

● Key words in the question signpost what data and calculations you need in order to work out the correct answer.

▶

- If you don't understand a question on first reading, read it again carefully. Still stuck? Move on to the next question.
- Watch out for nonsensical answers.

You will need to work quickly and accurately, but if you run out of time it's not the end of the world – often the test does not expect you to answer every question. Use these techniques to power through and maximise success.

brilliant dos and don'ts

Do

✓ Take a moment to look at the data to get a sense of what it is telling you before you tackle the questions.

✓ Check you understand what the question wants you to do; key words in the question will signpost you.

✓ Check what units are used in the tables against what unit is required for the answer, as they can often be different.

✓ Feel confident that you can do the maths; the calculations aren't too complex.

Don't

✗ Linger or agonise – if you are stuck, just move calmly on to the next question.

✗ Leave any of the questions unanswered; if you are pushed for time make an educated guess.

5.5 What does an inductive/abstract/ diagrammatic reasoning test look like?

The question format is a series of diagrams or pictures, normally five in a sequence. These are spread out on the same line, going across a page. Underneath the test sequence, you are given another set of (usually five) diagrams or pictures from which you have to select the correct answer. An alternative format use is multiple choice answers, where you are given a handful of possible answers to choose from. There are no numbers involved in these tests. Words aren't involved either, except in the instructions which are actually pretty minimal: typically *What comes next in the sequence?*

brilliant tips

● Inductive tests use your reasoning skills to deduce which image fits into a sequence.

● You might have to predict which comes next in a sequence or identify which image fits earlier in a sequence.

● Using reason and logic you will puzzle out the rules which govern the way the images change in a sequence.

● You will also use creativity and flexibility when testing out whether your rules apply.

● All the information you need is there in the diagrams.

● You can make sense of the most baffling images if you look beyond the pictures to the underlying rules.

Underlying every abstract reasoning test question are rules which govern how the shapes change one after the other. There may be only one or two rules at play, but they are rules which the shapes have to obey. You can also think of these rules as a relationship or pattern across the images. It would be unusual only to have one rule and generally you are looking for two or three rules; but it is only by working on the puzzle that you can be sure exactly how many rules are in play. The level of complexity of these tests can vary, but you can use the same tips and techniques regardless of how tricky they are.

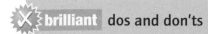 **brilliant dos and don'ts**

Do

✔ Look across the sequence of images for patterns and relationships.

✔ Expect there to be more than one rule in play.

✔ Look for increase, decrease, directional change, rotation, reflection and sequence.

✔ Eliminate answers systematically as you formulate each underlying rule.

Don't

✗ Panic if the rule isn't immediately obvious: reason it out.

✗ Forget to check the number of objects within each diagram.

5.6 What does a situational judgement test (SJT) look like?

The SJT is all words, which makes for a lot of reading. Typically, the SJT starts by outlining the job role you are to imagine yourself doing – trainee hotel manager or civil servant, for example. You are then given a situation; sticking with the examples just given, it could be that you are duty manager for the day, or that you have to brief a minister before a public meeting. Next follows a series of situations, again relating back to that job role in that situation – someone asks you to give them a discounted room rate, or the local news reports warn of feelings running high in advance of the public meeting. Finally, you are given a range of possible responses to that situation; four answer options is typical. There are a couple of variations in terms of what you are instructed to do at this point: either choose what you would be most likely to do, or choose which option would be most effective. There are also a couple of variations in the answer format: either you choose one answer or you rate all of the answers in rank order. It's all about your judgement.

brilliant tips

- Take on the role depicted, put yourself in the frame and take decisions as if you were actually doing that job.

- Read through all the answer options, giving each one due consideration before making your decisions.

- If you're torn between two answers, go with your first instinct and move on to the next challenge.

- Be aware that this is a test of your thinking and judgement; stay focused on the task throughout.

Is there a right answer?

In contrast to all the reasoning tests, there is not one correct answer to the SJT questions. There is, however, one answer which the test is looking for. That is the course of action which works most effectively, according to the company's values. Companies and organisations are very open about their values, because they want to attract employees who will work with their ethos and culture. You can readily locate this information in their promotional literature or on their websites. It may be listed under different headings, such as core values, competencies, mission statement or vision.

brilliant dos and don'ts

Do

- ✔ Imagine yourself doing the role described.
- ✔ Check out the organisation's values and vision.
- ✔ Check whether to choose or rank your answers.

▶

> **Don't**
> X Panic if you've never had experience in the role.
> X Latch onto or dismiss any one answer until you have considered them all.
> X Over-think your answers – trust your instinctive choice.

5.7 What do personality tests look like?

You'll be presented with a series of written questions or statements. Tests vary in length from around 20 items to more than 60 items. Duration therefore varies too, from 15 to 60 minutes. It is only in very specific tests that you'd be given any images to interpret, so you can expect to read through a series of questions or statements.

What do personality tests feel like?

In all the reasoning tests, you are set a problem to which there is only one correct answer; your task is to work that out. With the situational judgement tests there is also one preferred answer; usually the one that is most effective in moving the situation forward in line with the organisation's values and mission. With personality tests, there is no right or wrong answer. It's a measure of the mind and it's all about you.

How to tackle a personality test

You may find it hard to keep focused on the test simply because it doesn't make explicit demands of working out as in the reasoning tests. Equally, you may feel anxious, worried that you have to match up to an ideal personality type. You might also find yourself stuck on a question because you can't quite see yourself in that situation; it can help in this case to think of what you would do in a work situation and answer from that perspective. The best tactic is to stay alert and give yourself up to the test, confident that by doing so you will probably enhance your self-knowledge.

brilliant tips

- Doing a personality test gives you valuable self-knowledge.
- Relax; the questions are not designed to trip you up.
- Stay true to yourself and give authentic answers.
- If in doubt, assume the question wants a work context response.
- Stay alert, particularly if you sense there is some repetition.
- Don't agonise – there really isn't a right answer here.

5.8 Where are you taking the tests?

At a venue – assessment centre or employer's premises

Check out where the test venue is and how to get there. Leave more time than you expect the journey to take. If you get there early, walk around the block before you go in and take a few deep breaths to steady yourself.

Online

It is most likely that you'll take the test online. It is worth checking that your PC matches the specification for online tests. Alternatively, book a computer at your university or local library.

Once you log on to start the tests, the time starts to count down; you'll need every second of that time allocation, so make sure nobody disturbs or distracts you. Log out of everything else and make it clear you're not to be disturbed.

5.9 Panicking and cheating

Even if you are really starting to feel desperate in your last-minute panic, don't even think about getting someone else to do your online tests for you. Even if you did get through, the next stage is likely to include verification tests, which would expose the deception, and no employer rates cheating. Even if, by some miracle, you faked your way into a job, it wouldn't be a good psychometric fit for you, so you'd only have cheated yourself. All you can do is give it your best shot this time, and if things don't work out, prepare better for next time.

 **practice**

The test of what you've grasped in this emergency chapter is taking a test for real. Here's a final recap of strategies and techniques. Good luck – and remember the rest of the text is here once you come back.

brilliant recap

- Most tests are taken online. Using the specification, check your PC is up to the task.
- Online tests can have a built-in timer, which can be off-putting; try to see it as a helpful reminder.
- If you're flummoxed by a question, breathe out slowly and read it again.
- If you're still stuck, move on to the next question.
- Generally speaking, any answer is better than no answer.
- No employer rates cheating: don't go there.

PART 2

Psychometric
tests

CHAPTER 6

Verbal reasoning tests

 learning

By the end of this chapter you will:

1   understand what the questions in verbal reasoning tests are asking you to do

2   have a clear strategy to minimise your stress so you can tackle the test and maximise your performance in verbal reasoning.

6.1 What does verbal reasoning actually test?

The questions in a verbal reasoning test demand you use reason and logic. To do that, you do of course need to read carefully. It is very important to focus entirely on the text you are given, and to be very disciplined, making absolutely sure that anything you deduce from your reading of the text can be backed up by a specific point which is there, for anyone to see, in the text. You have to pinpoint the evidence which supports the statement you choose, whether that's true or false. That kind of discipline and narrow focus on the exact text in front of you is what gives you the possibility of stating that it's impossible to say. So in forcing you to choose one of the three possible answers (True, False, Cannot say), the test can see whether you search for evidence, locate it and have justified confidence in the conclusion you reach.

'Try to determine the necessary and sufficient conditions that the question is asking for. Only if they are satisfied should a positive or negative answer be given – as opposed to Can't say.'

Ed, BSc Psychology, Politics and Economics

6.2 Why do employers use verbal reasoning tests?

Employers want to know how you tackle problems, and whether you work systematically through a problem to reach a conclusion which is both considered and logical. Verbal reasoning does this using data presented in words. Employers want to know that you can handle complex ideas and make sense of data by examining it closely and checking that, in so doing, you aren't jumping to conclusions or assuming something that isn't explicitly backed up by what it there in the text. Although you do have to be able to understand what you are reading, this kind of testing goes beyond English comprehension. It satisfies employers that you will look carefully at data, and use logic and reason to work out what conclusions can be drawn. This is a skill which is needed in many different jobs across a range of sectors. So the use of verbal reasoning tests in selection is widespread.

 **brilliant** definition

Verbal reasoning
Verbal reasoning goes beyond straightforward English comprehension, to test how you reach a justifiable conclusion by making sense of written data, using logic and reason.

6.3 What does a verbal reasoning test look like?

What can you expect from a verbal reasoning test? Typically you will be presented first with a piece of text. It won't necessarily be a long piece, maybe only a paragraph or two. What then follows is a set of statements. Your task is to decide for each statement whether that statement is: (a) true, (b) false or (c) impossible to say. Examples of verbal reasoning tests are included in this chapter; first off you'll read an example question and be shown how the correct answer is worked out. Then there'll be another question for you to have a go at before you're shown how the correct answer is worked out. Finally, when you are ready, you can take an entire verbal reasoning test on your own, in your own time. You'll find this in Part 3, Brilliant practice. You can then check the answers in Part 4, Brilliant answers to see how you get on.

 recap

> Later in this chapter there will be an example which is worked
> through for you. Then you'll try a practice question on your own, and
> again, you'll be taken step by step through the working out. Finally,
> you'll do a whole test on your own, in your own time. Answers will
> be provided!

6.4 How to tackle a verbal reasoning test

Examine the text systematically to find the answer

Although you will, of course, need to understand the paragraph,
a verbal reasoning test is not simply checking your English comprehension. It is testing how you use reason to puzzle out the
correct solution to a problem. Part of that testing (of how well
you reason) is to see if you make assumptions; that is, whether
you bring into your reasoning something which isn't actually
there in the text. So the very first thing you do is read the text,
read the question and then go back to the text to work through
it systematically to find the answer.

 tip

> Help your concentration by reading the text out loud or under your
> breath.

Verbal reasoning does not test your prior knowledge

You may come across a passage which relates to a topic you
already know something about; being familiar with the subject
might make you feel rather more confident about tackling it. But
beware – it is not your knowledge that is being tested, but your

ability to understand what the text does and does not tell you. You have to focus hard on the text and equally hard on the questions, taking care to ensure that you don't go beyond what the text says, or beyond exactly what the questions ask. Recognising a familiar subject can give you false confidence; remember to let go of all your background knowledge and stick doggedly to the text in front of you.

brilliant tip

Be particularly careful if the passage you're being tested on refers to a subject you have some knowledge of. It is really easy to assume something is in the text because you are familiar with it. But unless it is there in the text you can't use it.

Pinpointing where in the text the answer comes from

Another reasoning error is when you infer something which is not implied by the text. You can check for this by re-reading the text once you've reached what you think is your conclusion, to make absolutely sure that you can reach that conclusion from the information there in front of you. If you can't pinpoint exactly where in the text you've drawn your conclusion from, it probably won't stand up. However, if you can deduce it by working step by step both through what the text says and then how you have made sense of it in order to reach a conclusion, you are probably on the right track.

brilliant tip

Once you think you've reached a conclusion, just go back into the text and identify where exactly you have found the bit that backs up your thinking. That should help you follow a logical reasoning process.

6.5 Working through verbal reasoning questions one step at a time

Having talked you through the principles behind tackling a verbal reasoning test, let's have a look at an example. All the examples in this chapter are published by Assessment Day, which has given permission for them to be used in this text. Read the paragraph through once.

Oil sands are most commonly found in Venezuela's Orinoco Basin and Alberta, Canada. Modern technology has made the extraction of crude bitumen, or unconventional oil, from these oil sands much easier. The crude oil that is extracted from traditional oil wells is a free-flowing mixture of hydrocarbons, whereas oil sands yield a highly viscous form of petroleum. Increasing world demand for oil and higher petrol prices have made the economic viability of extracting oil sands approach that of conventional oil.

Oil sands have been described as one of the dirtiest sources of fuel. Compared to conventional oil, four times the amount of greenhouse gases are generated from the extraction of bitumen from oil sands. Additionally, there is an impact on the local environment. Tailing ponds of toxic waste are created whenever the tar sands are washed with water.

Proponents of oil sands development point to the land that has already been reclaimed following oil sands development. Also, that there will be considerably less surface impact once technology innovations have allowed oil sand reserves to be drilled rather than mined.

Don't panic if the text is on something very unfamiliar to you

Don't worry if you have no idea about oil sands or energy extraction; all you need to answer the questions is there in the text in front of you. Your challenge is to focus hard on the text, then work your way through it logically for evidence to support your choice of answer to each of the questions set.

Don't relax if the text is on something very familiar to you

Equally, if you are the world's expert on oil sands, leave all your prior knowledge behind. All you need to answer the questions is there in the text in front of you. Your challenge is to focus hard just on the text, working your way through it logically for evidence to support your choice of answer to each of the questions set.

Working through the question one step at a time

So far, so good? Your task now is to consider five statements and work out, for each one, if it is 'True', 'False' or 'Cannot say'. Remember that 'Cannot say' doesn't just mean you don't have a clue so you've opted for that answer. 'Cannot say' means that there is nothing in the text which can justify either 'True' or 'False' as an answer.

Here's your first statement:

Q1 **Oil sands offer a clean solution for meeting future energy needs.**

Now you've got the statement, go back into the text and read it through. In this, your first practice, you're only looking for a justification for either 'True' or 'False'; 'Cannot say' isn't the answer here.

Is this statement true? No, it isn't. The first line of the second paragraph tells us that: 'Oil sands have been described as one of the dirtiest sources of fuel'. No way is that a clean solution for future energy needs; no way is that statement true. You've pinpointed exactly the supporting evidence you need, so you can confidently pick 'False' as the correct answer.

Try another:

Q2 **Oil sands are only found in Alberta and the Orinoco basin.**

Go back to the text and read it through again, this time looking for a justification for either 'True' or 'False', bearing in mind that if you can't find anything in the text to support either of these, the correct answer might therefore be 'Cannot say'. Only the first paragraph mentions locations for oil sands so that's where the answer is going to be. It says 'Oil sands are most commonly found in Venezuela's Orinoco Basin and Alberta, Canada'. Does that mean the statement is true? Not quite. The statement specifies that oil sands are 'only' found in Alberta and the Orinoco Basin – but the text states that oil sands are 'most commonly' found there. 'Most commonly' does not mean the same as 'only' so the statement is not true, which means that 'False' is the correct answer. This shows that you do have to think logically, really respecting the confines of the statement and how it relates to its corresponding text. Keep that in mind as you try another.

One more example question:

Q3 **Bitumen is a highly viscous form of petroleum that needs to be heated to flow.**

There's nothing in the second or third paragraph about this, so the first paragraph is where we need to concentrate. The second sentence confirms that 'oil sands yield a highly viscous form of petroleum' but there is nothing in there about heating. There is nothing in the text which confirms the statement, nor is there anything which disproves the statement. We can't therefore say that the statement is true, nor can we say it is false. The only answer we can give is 'Cannot say', which is of course the correct answer.

 **tip**

Remember that all the information you need is in the text in front of you – it's a reasoning test, not a general knowledge quiz.

Almost the last question for you to try:

Q4 **It is almost as expensive to extract oil sands as conventional oil.**

You have to dig deeper for the correct answer here because there is nothing explicit in the text about the expense of extracting. What you can do is to infer from the text – that is, you put together what you do know and can logically reach a conclusion about what that means. It is not explicit in the text but you can pick it up. Here's how. Paragraphs 2 and 3 have nothing about expense or cost so they don't help us with this question. Paragraph 1 includes a description of the process and the locations, and the final sentence in this paragraph does talk about 'viability'. We know we are looking for something about cost so we should pick up on 'viability' because that's a measure of whether something is worth the cost. The key sentence is: 'Increasing world demand for oil and higher petrol prices have made the economic viability of extracting oil sands approach that of conventional oil'. It is reasonable to deduce from this that if higher prices for petrol have made the economic viability of extracting from oil sands approach the economic viability of conventional oil, then the cost incurred with oil sands is getting closer to the cost incurred with conventional oil. So the statement is true.

Last question on this paragraph:

Q5 **Extracting bitumen from conventional oil generates four times the level of greenhouse gases than extracting from oil sands.**

Paragraph 2 is the one for this question, with explicit reference to greenhouse gases. The bit about 'four times the amount of greenhouse gases' jumps out at you. Stop! Double check what the statement actually says: 'Extracting bitumen *from conventional oil* generates four times the level of greenhouse gases than extracting from oil sands'. Compare that with the paragraph which says: 'four times the amount of greenhouse gases are generated from the extraction of bitumen *from oil sands*'. The statement is in fact the opposite of the paragraph and it is therefore false.

6.6 Strategies used in tackling these questions

Having worked through the questions and the reasoning behind the answers, you now have a handful of techniques which you can keep using to tackle any verbal reasoning test. Take a moment to reflect on how you got through the questions and see how many of the strategies you've already used just in this first practice.

 recap

- You read the text carefully to get an overview, then read it very specifically to test out whether the answer statement is 'True', 'False' or 'Cannot say'.

- You focused on each statement one at a time, not drifting off, but sticking with the question in front of you.

- Each time you went back into the text it was purely to answer the question you were considering at that time.

- Even when the answer seems obvious, you've gone back to make quite sure your reasoning is sound and you can justify your chosen answer.

- You didn't panic that the subject of the text was completely unknown to you.

- You didn't jump to conclusions because you already knew something about the subject of the text.

- You can pinpoint exactly where in the text the justification for your choice of answer lies.

6.7 Practise your verbal reasoning on these questions

As you know, with a verbal reasoning test, your task is to consider a set of statements (which relate to a text you are given to read) then work out, for each statement if it is 'True', 'False' or

'Cannot say'. Practise again, by reading the following text and working through the five questions, using these techniques.

brilliant recap

- Read the text first for overview, then re-read it for each statement you have to decide on.

- Focus on one question at a time; justify that one then start afresh on the next.

- If the answer jumps out at you, take a moment to double check your reasoning is sound.

- 'Cannot say' has to be justified in the same way as 'True' or 'False'.

- You know that the answer is in the text so you look closely.

- If you are really stuck, you move on.

The legal term double jeopardy refers to a second prosecution of an individual for an offence for which he has already been prosecuted. Double jeopardy is famously prohibited in the Fifth Amendment of the United States constitution, which states that no person shall, 'be subject for the same offence to be twice put in jeopardy of life or limb.' Not only does the double jeopardy doctrine uphold the finality of criminal proceedings, it also protects individuals from the stress of multiple prosecutions. Despite dating back to Roman times, this legal rule is often challenged. Some legal reform advocates believe that a second trial should be permitted if significant new evidence becomes available – for example DNA evidence can reveal more using more recent technology.

Double jeopardy laws are intended to protect innocent people from continual harassment by the state. They also prevent a defendant from receiving successive trials for the same offence – for instance, someone found guilty of murder cannot also be tried for manslaughter for the same act. Some exceptions exist. A new trial is allowed if the original trial is declared a mistrial, or if an appeal against a conviction is successful. The rules also do not restrict a different sovereignty from prosecuting for the same offence. Similarly, in the United States, civil proceedings can be brought against someone who has already been acquitted or convicted of committing the offence.

Q1 **Under double jeopardy rules, someone who has been acquitted of a crime can never be retried for the same offence.**

True   False   Cannot say

Q2 **Criminal and civil proceedings fulfil different objectives in the United States.**

True   False   Cannot say

Q3 **Double jeopardy laws exist to prevent the government from persecuting innocent individuals.**

True   False   Cannot say

Q4 **New technology can shed new light on old cases.**

True   False   Cannot say

Q5 **The double jeopardy rule was first expressed in the Fifth Amendment of the United States Constitution.**

True   False   Cannot say

Working through the answer for 'double jeopardy' verbal reasoning questions

Q1 **Under double jeopardy rules, someone who has been acquitted of a crime can never be retried for the same offence.**

The second sentence of the first paragraph would seem to support this statement but you have to check the whole text to be sure there isn't something in there which presents a competing alternative.

You'll find it in the second paragraph, which states that 'Some exceptions exist'. If there are possible exemptions, the claim that someone can 'never' be retried doesn't stand up. So the statement is false.

Q2 Criminal and civil proceedings fulfil different objectives in the United States.

Civil proceedings are mentioned in the final sentence of the second paragraph, but only in relation to double jeopardy. There is nothing here or anywhere else in the text that supports the above statement. Which means we cannot say.

brilliant tip

Remember that the answer 'Cannot say' means that there is nothing in the text which can justify either 'True' or 'False' as the answer. You still have to find the reason for 'Cannot say'.

Q3 Double jeopardy laws exist to prevent the government from persecuting innocent individuals.

The opening sentence of paragraph two states clearly that 'double jeopardy laws are intended to protect innocent people from continual harassment by the state'. That's the reason this statement is true.

Q4 New technology can shed new light on old cases.

The final sentence of the first paragraph refers to DNA testing as an example of new technology which can reveal more evidence on an old case. So this statement is true.

Q5 The double jeopardy rule was first expressed in the Fifth Amendment of the United States Constitution.

Quick reading shows that the Fifth Amendment does indeed prohibit double jeopardy. However, this statement refers to when the double jeopardy rule was *first* expressed. The third sentence of the first paragraph tells us the rule dates back to 'Roman times' so we know it was in enshrined in law rather earlier. Which leads to the conclusion that this statement is false.

 practice

Now check that you understand what verbal reasoning is asking you to do by trying the Chapter 6 practice verbal reasoning test (in Part 3, Brilliant practice). Check that you are using the brilliant tips here as strategies for tackling verbal reasoning tests.

---

brilliant dos and don'ts

Do

✔ Read the text carefully.

✔ Read each question carefully.

✔ Identify what it is in the text that you have used as the justification for your answer.

Don't

✗ Jump to conclusions.

✗ Bring in any prior knowledge – stick to the text given.

✗ Choose 'Cannot say' as a default answer.

CHAPTER 7

Numerical or non-verbal reasoning tests

brilliant learning

By the end of this chapter you will:

1 understand what the questions in non-verbal/numerical reasoning tests are asking you to do

2 have a clear plan of attack to minimise your stress so you can maximise your performance in non-verbal reasoning.

7.1 What does numerical/non-verbal reasoning actually test?

Non-verbal reasoning tests focus on your use of reason and logic, to make sure that you can reach a justifiable conclusion by making sense of the information given, then working through a problem systematically, using reason and logic. 'Non-verbal' is used partly to distinguish these tests from verbal tests, but using 'non-verbal reasoning' as a label indicates that the test is not just about numbers but about using reason to work through a problem which is data based.

brilliant definition

Numerical and non-verbal reasoning tests
Numerical and non-verbal reasoning tests focus on your ability to use reason and logic on data presented as numbers and figures.

7.2 Why do employers use numerical/ non-verbal tests?

Employers use numerical tests to see how you approach numerical problems and how you handle figures. Understanding whether profits are going up or down, or whether the wage bill can be paid from this month's income are everyday challenges in business. So understanding numbers matters. Non-verbal reasoning is important right across the board because any company, large or small, profit-making or charitable, start-up or well established, has to make ends meet.

Employers usually provide an example of the test format they use so that you know what to expect; you can normally find this on the employer's website or on their recruitment literature. They may well be explicit about which test publisher they use so you can pinpoint exactly which you are going to encounter. That said, all non-verbal reasoning tests are doing the same job so just get practising – get your head round what is being tested and you will easily cope with test variants.

brilliant tip

Ask the employer or look at their website to check what test format they actually use.

7.3 Test formats can vary

The precise format of the test can vary, although all test the same numerical reasoning skill set. The practice questions included here will help you prepare for all kinds of numerical test, but make sure you check how the questions will be presented for the test you are taking.

What if maths isn't my top skill?

If you feel that maths is not your strong point, do not panic! The level of maths required is not impossibly high. Unlike a lot of the maths you learn at school, the maths necessary for these tests tends to be applicable to real-life situations, which is why employers want people who can do them. You do need to understand percentages and ratios and you will need to do arithmetic – for which you might find some GCSE level revision guides useful, along with the practice and explanations in this text. Remember that what lies at the heart of these tests is how you reason and solve problems and that's what you need to get hold of.

 recap

Numerical reasoning tests are used very widely by employers because they want to be sure you understand numerical data used in everyday work, no matter what kind of sector you're working in.

7.4 What to expect and how to prepare

What does a numerical test look like?

Numerical reasoning tests follow a pretty standard format. There will be a chunk of numerical data which could be presented as a graph, or in a table, or as a combination of the two. You will then have to use the data to answer a question, or series of questions, by choosing the correct answer in a multiple choice format.

You will, of course, need some basic maths skills, and the best way to bring these up to scratch is to practise before you take the test. Some people find that going back to their GSCE revision books is the most helpful thing they can do. Apart from basic arithmetic, you will need to be confident about calculating percentages, fractions and ratios. You'll also need to be familiar with different types of graph, whether that's a line graph, a bar or pie chart for example. Generally you won't be tested on more 'conceptual' mathematical questions such as geometry or complex algebra, unless of course you are applying for a job in which these skills are essential (engineering, for example).

What does a numerical test feel like?

Your task is to recognise what the data represents, understand what the question is asking for, and identify which data points you need in order to calculate the correct answer – all within a set time limit. This can be off-putting, especially when confronted with a combination of complex data, but remember that these tests are designed to make you feel pressurised because employers want to measure how you perform in that condition.

'Psychometrics are no fun, but they're not meant to be.'

Hannah, BSc Economics and Politics

You will need to work quickly and accurately, but if you run out of time it's not the end of the world; often the test design does not expect you to answer every single question. In any case, this chapter will help you develop a strategy to power through and maximise success.

brilliant tip

Don't worry if you don't answer every single question in the time given, but do use your time well.

7.5 Plan of attack

Familiarise yourself with the data

When you're up against the clock it can be tempting to scan over the data and concentrate on the question, but that can lead to oversights and silly mistakes. You shouldn't spend too long on the data, but it is important to grasp what story it is telling; what the various columns in a table mean or how the bars in a bar chart relate to one another. It's also a good idea to have a look at units and orders of magnitude (e.g. 'in thousands' or 'per capita') as these can easily trip you up and lead to a wrong answer.

Read the question

This sounds obvious, but when you're nervous and under pressure it's easy to misinterpret what the question is actually asking. Take a deep breath and read the question over a couple of times. Again be especially careful with regard to units. There are key words in the question which signpost you to what you need to do; the first practice question shows you what to look out for.

brilliant tip

Take a minute to read the question over a couple of times, noting the key words that signpost what you need to do to get to the correct answer.

Identify the data you need in order to answer the question

It is likely that you will need to work with several different pieces of information in order to answer the question. For the harder questions you will often need to use the data presented to generate a new piece of data which is essential to answering the question. For example if the question asks you to calculate a change in GDP (gross domestic product) and the table in front of you only gives you GDP per capita and population size, you'll need to multiply the two in order to give you the GDP figure necessary to answer the question.

brilliant tip

Don't be scared off by number formats you're not familiar with, such as exchange rates; the numerical skills involved remain the same.

If you don't get it, move on

It's horrible coming up against a question that you just don't get. But given that you are against the clock the best strategy is to put it behind you and move on to the next question, because you don't have time to waste figuring it out. This can also apply to questions that you know will take a lot of working out; better leave it until the end if you think you might be able to answer two other questions in the time it would take you to answer that tricky one. If the test format allows to you mark the question, do that by putting a cross next to it on the answer sheet. If you're taking the test online, note it down on some rough paper so that you can go back to it at the end of the test once you have aced all of the questions you knew how to do and have those in the bag. Make sure that you do select an answer though, even if you have to guess.

 **brilliant** timesaver

If you get stuck on a question, read it again carefully. If you still don't get it, move on.

Pick the right answer

With all the practice you've done you should be able to speedily and accurately perform the relevant calculations which will give you an answer that matches up with one of the multiple choices. If this isn't the case, make sure you are using the right units or that you have rounded up or down correctly according to the question.

Select an answer that makes sense

Be careful in selecting an answer that makes sense. If the question asks for how many cars, you need to look for a whole number because you can't have a bit of car, so you wouldn't pick a decimal answer (such as 15.1) because that answer doesn't make sense. Otherwise have a quick re-read of the question, and of the data, as you may have overlooked or misunderstood something. A quick re-read means just that – read it again carefully and if you don't get it, move on.

'Carefully read each question, don't rush, and then trust whatever you think is the right answer. Don't doubt yourself, it wastes time.'

Rishabh, BA Economics

Don't leave any question unanswered

Unless specified otherwise, in the vast majority of tests you are not penalised for a wrong answer. Since tests are multiple choice, even if you have no idea what the answer is or if you're running out of time, just pick an answer because at least you have a shot of picking up points. You can however increase the odds of your answer being correct if you have time. For example, if the question asks to calculate a percentage change, and three of the answers are increases and two are decreases, you might be able to see from the data that there was an increase even if you can't (or don't have time to) figure out the actual answer. Doing this increases your chances of picking the correct answer from 1 in 5 to 1 in 3.

brilliant tip

If you're stuck for an answer, don't just guess: narrow the options down to maximise your chances of guessing correctly.

Practice makes perfect

For numerical reasoning tests in particular, it is really important to practise if you want to maximise your chances of success. Especially if you haven't done any maths beyond GCSE equivalent, practising will help you to get back into the habit of working with numbers. If you're lacking in confidence then start small; do some simple percentage calculations or ratios to get your head around how the numbers interact with each other. There are plenty of online guides and practice for this, such as: **www.bbc.co.uk/education/subjects/z6pfb9q**. The aim is to get to a point where during the tests these calculations are second nature and all you really need to focus on is the particularities of the question. Furthermore, the more comfortable you are with numbers and with these basic calculations, the easier it will be to spot if you have made a mistake – you should make sure you know, for example, roughly what a 50% increase looks like.

'Once you've done enough practice tests, you will have encountered pretty much all of the questions that they can realistically ask you.'

Ed, BSc Politics, Philosophy and Economics

Develop a way of working out that makes sense to you

Try to develop a way of working out that makes sense to you; don't just memorise the steps because when you're under pressure or the data doesn't look familiar, it can fall to pieces. This being said, your way of working out also needs to be efficient. For example, when calculating a percentage change, most textbooks will tell you to multiply by 100 at the end. That's true in that the final figure will be correct, but in the test if you get to calculate a percentage change that gives 0.84, there is no need to waste time multiplying by 100 when it's clear that the answer is 84%.

 **recap**

- You need to handle percentages, fractions, ratios, differing units and to spot increases as opposed to decreases. You need to be able to make sense of graphs, tables, bar and pie charts.

- GSCE revision guides can help with all of these.

- Practise using a calculator and working out sums involved.

- Test formats can vary but test the same numerical reasoning skills.

- Tests are nearly always timed – every second counts, so having a plan of attack helps.

- Key words in the question signpost what data and calculations you need in order to work out the correct answer.

- Take a moment to look at the data to see what it tells you.

- If you don't understand a question at first reading, read it again carefully. Still stuck? Move on to the next question.

- Watch out for nonsensical answers.

7.6 Working through numerical reasoning test questions one step at a time

Having talked you through the principles behind tackling a numerical reasoning test, let's have a look at an example. All the examples in this chapter are published by Assessment Day which has given permission for them to be used in this text.

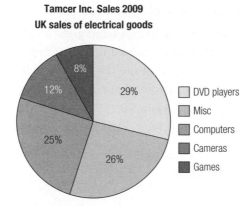

Tamcer Inc. Sales 2009
UK sales of electrical goods

- DVD players
- Misc
- Computers
- Cameras
- Games

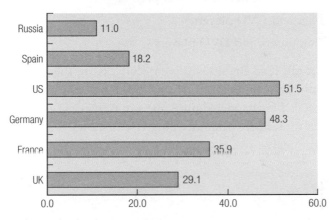

Tamcer Inc. - Sales 2009 (£100,000s)

Here's the first example of a numerical reasoning test question; work through it step by step, reading these notes to guide you. Before you even get to the question, look at the data.

Familiarise yourself with the data

Start by taking a moment to familiarise yourself with the data which is presented in a pie chart and a bar chart. Note that the bar chart presents sales in several countries (including the UK), while the pie chart presents a breakdown of sales just in the UK. There is therefore a link between the two sets of data and it is likely that the correct answer will require handling of both these data sets.

Note how the data sets relate to each other

The pie chart deals in percentages and gives no absolute figures, whereas the bar chart gives actual figures for sales. But putting the two together tells us what the UK sales actually are; the total UK bar in the bar chart shows that total UK sales (i.e. the whole pie chart) figure is £2,910,000 (29.1 × £100,000) – we will probably need to use this later. Here's your first question:

Q1 **In 2009, which categories of electrical goods each sold more than £0.75 million in the UK?**

(a) Misc

(b) Misc, Computers and DVD players

(c) Misc and DVD players

(d) Computers and DVD players

First of all, read the question carefully. Note the unit here is £million, even though the figures in the bar chart are units of £100,000. This happens quite often in numerical reasoning so be alert to it; apart from anything else it shows you can switch units and realise you're doing so.

> ### brilliant tip
>
> Note what units of measurement are used – hundreds, thousands, hundred thousands, millions. Often the data is presented in one unit and the test wants the answer in a different unit. Always do a quick check that you're working in the appropriate unit.

Key words in the question help you to identify the data you need

Once you understand what the question is asking, you can identify the data you need to work out the correct answer. The first hurdle therefore is to understand the question. The question itself offers clues in the form of key words. The key words in this example question are:

● *'In 2009...'* Note that both charts present figures from 2009.

● *'electrical goods'* Which are only in the pie chart, so that's going to be needed.

● *'in the UK'* Although both graphs include UK sales, the question asks about an actual figure, so the bar chart is also needed because the pie chart only shows percentages.

Doing the calculations step by step

Now it is clear what the question is asking, and that both sets of data are needed to work out the answer, it is just a question of working through it one step at a time. The calculations needed are pretty straightforward, but it helps to work through it systematically – and to understand why each step is necessary.

Step 1 – calculating the total UK sales figure

The bar chart gives total UK sales = $2.91 \times £100,000$ = $£2,910,000 = £2.91$ million. As the question demands a figure in £millions, stick to this unit.

brilliant tip

Convert the unit so you are working out in the unit the question demands.

Step 2 – calculating actual sales for each type

The pie chart (UK sales of electrical goods) gives the percentage sales breakdown for each category (e.g. cameras, DVD players). You need to calculate actual sales for each type by using the figure from Step 1, that is £2.91 million.

Computers: 25% of £2.91 million = $25 \div 100 \times 2.91$ million
$$= 0.7275 \text{ million}$$

It is worth noting here that these tests are done against the clock, so you should think about shortcuts. When you are typing figures into the calculator, don't waste time typing all the zeroes for the millions. As long as you are consistent throughout the different categories you can just find the percentage of 2.9. You do have to remember that the answer should be in millions so you need to recognise that 0.7275 means 0.7275 million. Try doing it during your practice sessions and it will soon become automatic. Even though it only saves seconds, sometimes you need all the time you can get to make sense of what the question is asking you to do. Once you're clear on that, the calculations are fairly straightforward. So it is worth saving precious seconds for the all-important reasoning process.

 brilliant timesaver

When typing figures into your calculator you don't have to type in all the zeroes for millions, so long as you are consistent across the categories and recognise the final answer should be in millions.

Step 2 – still calculating actual sales for each type
Use the same approach for all the different categories as follows:

DVD players: 29% of £2.91 million = 29 ÷ 100 × 2.91 million
= 0.8439 million

Cameras: 12% of £2.91 million = 12 ÷ 100 × 2.91 million
= 0.3492 million

Step 2 – still calculating actual sales but using reason to eliminate options
You've now got the chance to save yourself a bit of time and effort. You know that you are looking for a category which sold more than 0.75 million. And you've just worked out that 12% of 2.91 million is less than 0.75 million (the Cameras calculation). It follows that 8% cannot be higher than 0.75 million and

therefore there you can eliminate the next option (the Games option) without having to perform the calculation. It is included here anyway so you can see how that works.

Misc: 26% of £2.91 million = 26 ÷ 100 × 2.91 million
= 0.7566 million

Games: 8% of 2.91 million = 8 ÷ 100 × 2.91 million
= 0.2328 million

brilliant **timesaver**

Save time where you can by skipping needless calculations.

Final step – identifying the correct answer
Now you know which categories sold more than £0.75 million, you can identify the correct answer:

(c) Misc and DVD players

Using reasoning to streamline your working

Working through every one of the five categories of goods included in the pie chart to calculate the actual sales figures was good practice. But it would have been reasonable to skip a couple of these calculations. Look back at the answer options. They are made up of only three categories – Misc, Computers and DVD players – so actually there is no need to do the calculations for Games or Cameras at all.

brilliant **timesaver**

Save time where you can by eliminating calculations which don't fit the answer options.

7.7 Working through another test question on the same data set

Here's the next question on the same data set:

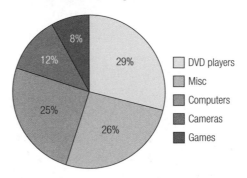

Tamcer Inc. Sales 2009
UK sales of electrical goods

- 29% DVD players
- 26% Misc
- 25% Computers
- 12% Cameras
- 8% Games

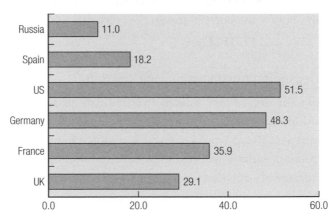

Tamcer Inc. - Sales 2009 (£100,000s)

Russia	11.0
Spain	18.2
US	51.5
Germany	48.3
France	35.9
UK	29.1

Q2 **The total worldwide sales for Tamcer Inc. are £29 million. What level of sales is accounted for by countries other than those shown?**

(a) £19.6 million

(b) £9.6 million

(c) £10.6 million

(d) £9.4 million

Key words in the question help you to identify the data you need

The question is asking about worldwide sales, so the bar chart has the necessary data. Note that both the question and the answer options are in £millions but the table is in £100,000s, so you need to be careful with units.

Doing the calculations step by step

Step 1 – calculating the sales of countries shown in the graph

The question is essentially asking for the difference between total sales and sales of the countries shown in the graph, which will give us the sales accounted for by other countries. You know that total sales are £29 million, so next you just need to calculate sales of countries shown in the graph:

UK (29.1) + France (35.9) + Germany (48.3) + US (51.5) + Spain (18.2) + Russia (11) = 194

Step 2 – converting the calculation into the right units for the answer

The table is in units of £100,000 but the question and possible answers are expressed in £millions so we need to convert the total sales into millions:

194 × £100,000 = £19.4 million

 **tip**

Convert the unit so you are working out in the right unit for the answer.

Step 3 – calculating the difference
Now you have the two figures you need, just calculate the difference:

£29 million − £19.4 million = £9.6 million.

Final step – identifying the correct answer
So the correct answer is (b) £9.6 million.

 **timesaver**

Don't type in all the zeroes. Just type 29 - 19.4 into the calculator and add the million back at the end.

7.8 Working through test questions on a different data set, step by step

Tze Motor Cars - Accounts (2006–2010)

	2010	2009	2008	2007	2006
Sales	£1,047.9m	£761.9m	£1,005.0m	£627.7m	£637.8m
Car units sold	16,710	12,636	15,905	12,163	12,360
Average sales price (per car)	£62,709	£60,296	£63,188	£51,607	£51,602
Average production costs (per car)	£14,500	£15,800	£13,600	£11,400	£13,750
Annual service charge per car	£250	£300	£350	£275	£400

Familiarise yourself with the data

Have a quick glance over the figures in the table, noticing that the columns represent years with the most current first, and that there are figures for averages and figures for number of car units which we will probably have to work with to get some kind of total.

**Q1 If the average sales price for 2010 was 5% higher, but
the number of cars sold that year was 9% lower, by what
percentage would the sales revenue have decreased for 2010?**

(a) No change

(b) 3.50%

(c) 3.55%

(d) 4.45%

(e) 4.60%

Key words in the question help you to identify the data you need

What information do you need to be looking for? From the
question you know to look at: the *'Average sales price (per car)'*
row, the *'Car units sold'* row and the *'Sales'* row, which are all in
the 2010 column. Now work your way through the question.

Doing the calculations step by step

Step 1 – calculating the percentage increase

Calculate what the 5% increase is *'if the average sales price for
2010 was 5% higher'*. We know that the 2010 sales price was
£62,709, so:

$$5\% \text{ of } £62,709 = 5 \div 100 \times £62,709 = £3,135.45$$
$$£62,709 + £3,135.45 = £65,844.45$$

 **timesaver**

A quicker way is to calculate 105% of £62,709 = 105 ÷ 100 ×
£62,709 = £65,844.45.

Step 2 – calculating the number of cars sold

Calculate the decrease in the number of cars sold if *'the number
of cars sold that year was 9% lower'* using the Brilliant timesaver
shortcut just shown:

9% lower is the same as 91% of the original, so 91% of 16,710 = 91 ÷ 100 × 16,710 = 15,206.1, but obviously, it's not possible to sell 0.1 of a car so it is better to express this as 15,206.

In this question doing so doesn't actually make a difference to the final answer but it's worth keeping an eye out for things like this in other questions where it does matter.

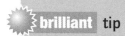 **tip**

Keep an eye out for nonsensical answers.

Step 3 – calculating the sales revenue
The calculation for sales revenue is price × quantity sold. Using the figures from step 1 and 2:

total sales revenue = £65,844.45 × 15,206 = £1,001,230,706.70

Step 3 – still calculating the sales revenue, but in millions
We need to compare this sales revenue figure to the sales revenue in 2010 which is expressed in millions, so note that £1,001,230,706.70 = £1,001.2307067 million.

Step 4 – calculating the decrease in sales revenue as a percentage
Next is to calculate the decrease in sales revenue from 2010 as a percentage, so:

$$1,047.9 - 1,001.2307067 = 46.6692933$$

But as all figures are in millions you can take the millions out.

$$46.6692933 ÷ 1,047.9 = 0.044536 × 100$$

Final step – identifying the correct answer
The answers are given to two decimal places so the correct answer is (d) 4.45%.

 **timesaver**

Calculate $1,001.2307067 \div 1,047.9 = 0.95546$ which is 95.546%, which is equivalent to a 4.45% decrease.

7.9 Working through another question on the car sales data, step by step

Tze Motor Cars – Accounts (2006–2010)

	2010	2009	2008	2007	2006
Sales	£1,047.9m	£761.9m	£1,005.0m	£627.7m	£637.8m
Car units sold	16,710	12,636	15,905	12,163	12,360
Average sales price (per car)	£62,709	£60,296	£63,188	£51,607	£51,602
Average production costs (per car)	£14,500	£15,800	£13,600	£11,400	£13,750
Annual service charge per car	£250	£300	£350	£275	£400

Q2 **In 2008, car sales were split across three equal-priced models in the ratio of 7:8:6 for models A, B and C respectively. What was the sales revenue for model A?**

(a) £287 million

(b) £335 million

(c) £382 million

(d) £383 million

(e) Can't tell from data

Key words in the question help you to identify the data you need

The question needs you to work with the 2008 column and the sales figures.

Step 1 – calculating what one unit is worth

The easiest way to deal with ratios is to divide by the total 'units' to find out what one 'unit' is worth. From this data set that would be:

$$7 + 8 + 6 = 21$$

The question tells us to look at car sales in 2008, which were £1,005.00m. So we divide that by the total 'units':

$$£1,005.00m \div 21 = 47.857m$$

Step 2 – calculating sales revenue for model A

The question asks for sales revenue for model A, which according to the ratio is 7 'units', so:

$$7 \times 47.857m = £334.99m$$

Final step – identifying the correct answer

The correct answer is therefore (b) £335 million.

Strategies used in tackling these questions

Having worked through the questions and the reasoning behind the answers, you now have a handful of techniques which you can keep using to tackle any numerical/non-verbal reasoning test. Take a moment to reflect on how you got through the questions and see how many of the strategies you've already used just in this first practice.

 **brilliant** recap

- You absolutely know how to work out a percentage, a percentage increase and a percentage decrease.

▶

- You know what ratios are and the importance of units in calculating ratios.
- You're confident about handling millions and 100,000s.
- You've thought about how to streamline your calculations.
- You've practised using a calculator.
- You've taken a moment to look at the data presented as graphs, tables or charts just to see what they are telling you.
- You've read the question carefully, noticing the key words that tell you what data and which calculations you need to work out the correct answer.
- You've watched out for different units in the data and in the answer options.
- You've translated from one unit to the other so it all lines up.
- You've estimated what the correct answer should be and have therefore dismissed nonsensical answer options.

7.10 Shaking things up – test formats can vary

The format of numerical reasoning tests does vary slightly, but they all test the same set of numerical reasoning skills. Your employer should give an indication of what format to expect, and it is good to familiarise yourself with the format you'll come up against so that you feel comfortable in tackling the questions. Below are two further numerical reasoning tests in slightly different formats. Don't let this put you off; you just need to work through them, step by step, in the same way you did the practice examples.

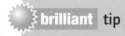 **brilliant** tip

Test formats vary but the numerical reasoning is constant, so just go for it, step by step.

7.11 Numerical critical reasoning

The style for these tests is different firstly in that there are many more answer options, which limits the merit of guessing. The example question given below offers 27 answers to choose from, which range from 386.15 to 388.75. Clearly, you will need to calculate the exact answer. Furthermore the time limit is per question, rather than overall – although this can only be reflected online and not on paper, it is worth bearing in mind.

Working through numerical critical reasoning test questions

Stocks and Shares ISA

Fund/asset	Number of units	Unit price
Global UT	3,394.640	106.40p
Worldwide Opp. UT	3,906.629	91.39p
UK Absolute Return	3,848.102	88.64p
Inv Grade Corp Bond UT	2,446.185	136.80p
Alternative Assets UT	3,028.983	107.00p
Mgd Equity and Bond UT	2,993.161	105.10p
Corporate Bond UT	1,553.360	202.30p
International UT	221.538	1,392.00p
UK Growth UT	1,819.186	97.47p

Current total value

Commencement date 29 October 2008

Total invested initially   £28,437

Total withdrawn

You decide to sell the holdings of Global UT and UK Growth UT at their current unit price. How many units of International UT shares can you afford to buy with the proceeds?

Key words in the question help you to identify the data you need

From the table you need to identify the holdings of Global UT and UK Growth UT, which are in the Number of units column, as well as their respective prices, which are in the Unit price column. You also need to identify the unit price of International UT shares in order to find out how many units you can afford with the money you've got from the proceeds.

Doing the calculations step by step

Step 1 – calculating what the Global UT and Growth UT shares are worth

There are 3,394.640 Global UT Shares at 106.40p each so 3,394.640 × 106.40p = £3,611.90

There are 1,819.186 UK Growth UT shares at 97.47p each so 1,819.186 × 97.47p = £1,773.16

Just be careful in converting from pence to pounds and rounding up correctly.

brilliant tip

If the number you are rounding is followed by 5, 6, 7, 8 or 9, you round the number up.

Step 2 – calculating the total revenue

Calculate total revenue: £3,611.90 + £1,773.16 = £5,385.06.

Step 3 – calculating how many International UT shares that would buy

You need to divide this total revenue figure by the price of International UT shares to work out how many you can afford, converting so that the unit price is in pounds too:

$$£5,385.06 \div £13.92 = 386.8578$$

Final step – identifying the correct answer
From the answers provided, the correct answer is 386.86.

 **tip**

Be careful when converting from pence to pounds and be careful about rounding up or down correctly.

7.12 Numerical comprehension

This type of question tends to be more wordy and, as the title suggests, makes you work harder to understand what calculations are required. Some numerical comprehension tests even use questions with answer options 'True', 'False' or 'Cannot say', which you will also find in verbal reasoning tests. You're developing the numerical reasoning skills you need, so that should hold no fear. In verbal reasoning tests, the key thing is to remember that you can only use the information contained in the words in front of you. Exactly the same applies in numerical reasoning. You can only use the information which is given to you for that question. You can't make assumptions, but need to pinpoint exactly what is in the text you are basing your understanding on. Everything you need for the correct answer is given to you; it's just a matter of working it out, step by step.

Working through numerical comprehension test questions

The distance between City A and City B is 178 km. Ricardo's car has a fuel economy of 35 miles to the gallon. If a litre of petrol costs £1.32, how much money would Ricardo spend on petrol travelling from City A to City B? (1 mile = 1.609344 kilometres; 1 gallon = 4.54609 litres).

(a) £16.78

(b) £18.96

(c) £20.10

(d) £22.93

(e) £25.83

Understanding the question

This question requires you to juggle various unit conversions –
but all the information you need is in the question, even if it is
not as clearly laid out as it would be in a table.

Step 1 – working out the distance travelled

In order to figure out how much it costs to get from A to B, you
need to know how much petrol Ricardo uses, and to do this you
need to know how far he travels. His fuel economy is given in
miles to the gallon but distance is given in kilometres, so to start
with you need to find this distance in miles using the conversion
rate given:

$$178 \text{ km} \div 1.609344 = 110.6040722 \text{ miles}$$

brilliant tip

> Remember that one mile is roughly one and a half kilometres, so a
> value in kilometres should always be higher than the value in miles.

Step 2 – working out how much petrol is used

Now you can calculate how many gallons of petrol are used:

$$110.6040722 \div 35 = 3.160116349 \text{ gallons}$$

However, the price of petrol is given by the litre, so you need to
convert these gallons to litres using the conversion rate you have
been given:

$$3.160116349 \times 4.54609 = 14.36617333 \text{ litres}$$

Step 3 – working out the petrol cost

Now you've got the units sorted you can calculate the cost of petrol in order to travel from City A to City B, by multiplying the volume of petrol used (in litres) by the price of petrol per litre:

$$14.36617333 \times £1.32 = £18.9633488$$

Final step – identifying the correct answer

Thus the correct answer is (b) £18.96.

Strategies used in tackling these questions

Having worked through the questions and the reasoning behind the answers step by step, you now have a handful of techniques which you can use to tackle any numerical reasoning test.

 **recap**

- Take a moment to look at the tables, graphs and charts first to see what they are telling you.

- Use the key words in the questions to signpost you to the relevant data and the necessary calculations.

- Keep an eye out for the use of different units – convert as needed.

- Make sure you can handle percentages, ratios and units.

- Streamline your working out so you save precious time.

- If you are really stuck, move on.

- Watch out for nonsensical answers either in the test or in your working out.

7.13 Practise your numerical reasoning

Now you've had a taste of what a numerical reasoning test will look like and how to approach the questions, work through the following four questions, then check your answers at the end.

Product code	Non-European stores selling product	Current month's sales ($)	Price per product unit ($)
DE45*	14	35,000	175
PU20*	9	20,000	200
AE25	6	13,000	130
PU10**	5	24,000	150
FD24**	7	9,000	180

*Promotional offer = 3 for the price of 2
**Promotional offer = 4 for the price of 3

Product code	European stores selling product	Current month's sales (€)	Price per product unit (€)
DE45	26	21,000	150
PU20	19	30,000	160
AE25	11	24,500	200
PU10	9	18,700	110
FD24	13	14,700	90

Q1 **What is the discrepancy (in $) between the AE25 price per product unit in non-European stores compared to European stores? Use an exchange rate of €0.80 to the $.**

(a) $30

(b) $120

(c) $130

(d) $200

(e) $230

Q2 **Given that a customer uses the promotional offers shown, put the 5 products sold in non-European stores into order of increasing promotional price per unit (starting with the cheapest).**

(a) AE25, PU10, DE45, FD24, PU20

(b) PU10, DE45, PU20, AE25, FD24

(c) PU10, DE45, AE25, PU20, FD24

(d) DE45, PU10, PU20, AE25, FD24

(e) PU10, DE45, PU20, FD24, AE25

Equity fund components (%)

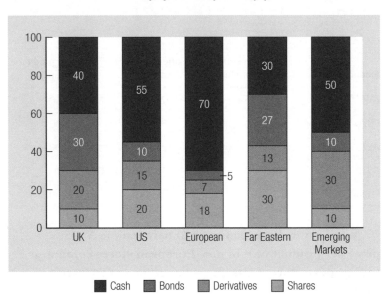

Equity fund values	UK	US	European	Far Eastern	Emerging Markets
Total value (£million)	55.6	24.3	52.1	26.2	38.9
Number of investors	3450	1460	3295	1575	2660

Q3 **On the previous day, the value of the cash held in the Emerging Markets Fund was 0.5% lower than the values given here. What was the previous day's value of cash in the Emerging Markets Fund?**

(a) £18.35 million

(b) £18.40 million

(c) £18.50 million

(d) £19.35 million

(e) £19.40 million

Q4 **Which equity fund has the highest average value per individual investor?**

(a) UK Fund

(b) US Fund

(c) European Fund

(d) Far East Fund

(e) Emerging Markets Fund

Working through the answers

Question 1

Question 1 asks for the discrepancy between non-European stores and European stores, which means that the information you need is in both tables. Note that it doesn't matter which is greater – the question only asks for the difference.

Step 1 From the table, AE25 price per product (non-European stores) = $130

Step 2 From the table AE25 price per product (European stores) = €200

Convert to $ using the exchange rate in the question: €200 ÷ 0.80 = $250

Step 3 Calculate the difference: $250 – $130 = $120

Thus the correct answer is (b) $120.

 **brilliant** tip

Don't be put off by exchange rates. Take an extreme example such as Zimbabwean dollars and pounds sterling which have very different strengths. You can see that the same product would cost a lot more Z$ than £. One currency will always be higher than another – even if that's not on such a big scale.

Question 2

Question 2 asks for products sold in non-European stores, so you need the first table.

Step 1 – Calculate the '3 for the price of 2' promotional offers:

DE45 promotional price per unit;
price for 2 without promotion = $175 \times 2 = \$350$;
so $\$350 =$ price for 3 with promotion, therefore price per unit with promotion = $\$350 \div 3 = \$116.67$

 **brilliant** timesaver

A quicker way to do this would be $\$175 \times 2/3 = \$116.67$

PU20 promotional price per unit $= 2/3 \times \$200 = \$133.33$

Step 2 – Calculate the 4 for the price of 3 promotional offers:

PU10 promotional price per unit $= 3/4 \times \$150 = \$112.50$

FD24 promotional price per unit $= 3/4 \times \$180 = \$135.00$

Step 3 – Put promotional prices in order with product AE25 which is not on promotion at $130, which gives you the correct answer (c) PU10, DE45, AE25, PU20, FD24.

Question 3

From the question we know to look for information in both the graph and the table, in particular looking at the Emerging Markets bar and column.

Step 1 – First you need to find the value of the cash in Emerging Markets equity fund using the data given. So £38.9 million × 50% = £38.9 million × 50/100 = £19.45 million.

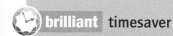 **timesaver**

50% of a number is the same as dividing by 2, just as 25% is the same as dividing by 4.

Step 2 – Calculate the previous day's value:

If the value was 0.5% lower, this just means you need to find 99.5% of the figure.

£19.45 million × 99.5/100 = £19.45 × 0.995 = £19.35 million, so the correct answer is (d) £19.35 million.

Question 4

The information you need is in the table. As there doesn't appear to be an obvious answer (in some cases there are answers that can obviously be ruled out by doing some quick mental calculations), you'll need to calculate each option.

Step 1 – Average value of equity fund per individual investor is just total value divided by number of investors, so:

UK: £55.6 million ÷ 3,450 = £16,116
US: £24.3 million ÷ 1,460 = £16,664
European: £52.1 million ÷ 3,295 = £15,812
Far Eastern: £26.2 million ÷ 1,575 = £16,635
Emerging Markets: £38.9 million ÷ 2,660 = £14,624

Thus the correct answer is (b) US Fund.

 practice

Now check that you understand what numerical/non-verbal reasoning is asking you to do, by trying the Chapter 7 practice non-verbal reasoning test in Part 3, Brilliant practice. Check that you are using these brilliant strategies for tackling verbal reasoning tests.

brilliant dos and don'ts

Do

✔ Check what units are used in the tables against what unit is required for the answer, as they can be different.

✔ Take a moment to look at the data to get a sense of what it is telling you before you tackle the questions.

✔ Check you understand what the question wants you to do – key words in the question will signpost you.

✔ Practise percentage and ratio calculations, using GCSE-level online revision and practice materials.

Don't

✗ Linger or agonise – if you are stuck, move on to the next question.

✗ Leave questions unanswered; if you are pushed for time make an educated guess.

CHAPTER 8

Inductive, abstract or diagrammatic reasoning tests

 **brilliant** learning

By the end of this chapter you will:

1 understand what the questions in inductive/abstract/diagrammatic reasoning tests are asking you to do

2 have a clear strategy to minimise your stress and maximise your performance in inductive reasoning.

8.1 What does inductive reasoning actually test?

Inductive, abstract or diagrammatic reasoning tests check that you can reach a justifiable conclusion by making sense of the information given, then working through a problem systematically, using reason and logic. Where verbal tests use words, and non-verbal tests use numbers and figures, inductive reasoning uses abstract shapes or diagrams. As with other reasoning tests, there is only one correct answer – your task is to work out the rules which will lead you to identify it. In common with other reasoning tests, you will be working within a time limit, so you need to use your time productively as you work against the clock. No prior knowledge is needed for this. Each set of diagrams obeys its own logic, according to its own rules. Nonetheless, doing some practice tests is advisable so that you know how to tackle the questions and can spend the precious time on working out answers.

brilliant recap

Later in this chapter there will be an example which is worked through for you. Then you'll try a practice question on your own, and again, you'll be taken step by step through the working out. Finally, you'll do a whole test on your own, in your own time. Answers will be provided!

'Make sure you do some practice questions beforehand to get your brain ticking over and so you are feeling sharp.'

Rishabh, BA Economics

8.2 Test formats can vary

A brief but important note on the different names in common use. Inductive reasoning tests are sometimes called abstract reasoning tests or diagrammatic reasoning tests. There are slight technical reasons for these differing names but they all test your ability to reason and you can tackle them all in the same way.

 definition

Inductive reasoning, abstract reasoning and diagrammatic tests
Inductive reasoning tests, abstract reasoning tests and diagrammatic reasoning tests are three different names for the same kind of test: how you analyse trends and relationships within a sequence of images by reasoning out the underlying rules.

8.3 Why do employers use inductive reasoning tests?

Although the tests themselves might not seem as obviously applicable in the workplace as verbal or numerical tests, the competencies that inductive reasoning tests measure are highly sought after by employers. Abstract reasoning tests measure your ability to analyse, by identifying relationships or trends, then applying what you have deduced to solve a problem.

Along with a readiness to work systematically through a problem, inductive reasoning demands a mindset which transfers readily to solving complex and unfamiliar problems in the workplace. This is all the more impressive when the problem at first sight appears baffling to the point of being nonsensical – as inductive tests can do to those new to them. So that is why employers use inductive reasoning tests: because the ability to solve a problem by working through it systematically and creatively is a valuable skill in every sort of business.

 **brilliant** tip

Abstract reasoning tests are used extensively in selection so you are highly likely to come across them.

8.4 What to expect and how to prepare

What does an inductive/abstract/diagrammatic reasoning test look like?

The question format is a series of diagrams or pictures, normally five in a sequence. These are spread out on the same line, going across a page. There are worked examples later in this chapter, so have a quick look there if you need help envisaging the format. Underneath the test sequence, you are given another set of (usually five) diagrams or pictures from which you have to select the correct answer. That's not very different from a multiple choice format where you are given a handful of possible answers to choose from. There are no numbers involved in these tests. Words aren't involved either, except in the instructions which are actually pretty minimal – typically: *What comes next in the sequence?*

brilliant tip

Inductive reasoning tests have multiple choice answers. All the questions and all the possible answers are all presented in diagrammatic form.

What do the answers look like?

The answer format is a series of diagrams or pictures, normally five in all. These appear to be very similar to each other although there will be distinguishing features. What distinguishes one picture from another will be a small but telling detail such as the number of objects, or the side on which there is shading or the orientation of a shape or its position in the frame. Only one of the answer diagrams obeys the rules which govern the question sequence. Your task is to use reason and logic to puzzle out what those rules are, then to apply those rules to the answer diagrams so as to identify the one which fits. Again, it can be hard to picture what this would look like. If you're struggling to imagine it, have a quick look at the examples included in this chapter.

 **tip**

If you're struggling to envisage what an inductive reasoning test looks like, have a quick look at the examples included in this chapter.

Question formats can vary

Asking for the 'next in the sequence' is a very common format for inductive reasoning tests; typically there are a handful of diagrams presented in a sequence, along with another set of diagrams from which you identify the next in the sequence, according to the rules you've deduced. However, abstract reasoning tests can appear in other formats, so instead of asking which image comes *next* in the sequence of five, one of the images within the sequence could be blanked out and you could be asked to deduce which image should go there; it could be the third in a sequence of five images. Regardless of the format, these kinds of tests all require the same skills and the same logical way of thinking.

 tip

> Question formats can vary but as the inductive reasoning skills
> remain the same, you can tackle them all.

Check out which format is used in the tests you are doing

Make sure that you check which test format you will be presented with for the job you are applying for, so that you can familiarise yourself with that particular format. The more comfortable you are with the question format, the quicker you can dive in and start answering the questions.

 tip

> Check out what format is used by the recruiter you are applying
> for; being familiar with the format helps you to concentrate on the
> thinking skills so you get on with the test.

What does an inductive/abstract/diagrammatic reasoning test feel like?

Inductive reasoning tests can be baffling the first time you come across them. At first sight, they can just look like a bunch of random shapes without any rhyme or reason. The question instructions are very minimal and simply throw you back onto the diagrams. That is because everything you need to know in order to answer the question is right there, before your very eyes, in that series of five diagrams. By the end of this chapter you'll know exactly what to expect in an inductive reasoning test and how to interpret those shapes. So you'll be able to tackle the questions, knowing what's expected and how to go about it. These tests do not require any prior knowledge, and indeed prior knowledge will not enhance your chances of success – although practice will.

'The reasoning test is testing you today, not when you were 16, not when you were 18. It is looking at who you are today.'

Sara Reading, Royal Bank of Scotland

What if I'm not the kind of person who naturally thinks in pictures?

If at this point you're starting to worry that you don't naturally express yourself in pictures (maybe you don't even doodle), don't worry. These tests aren't looking for visual thinking but for reasoning ability. In that sense, they are much closer to the verbal and non-verbal reasoning tests.

 brilliant definition

Inductive reasoning
Inductive reasoning is about how you work through a problem systematically, not about how you express yourself visually.

Specialist jobs where the ability to think in two and three dimensions is important (engineering for example) will use very specific tests. Jobs where visual thinking and expression are important (graphic design for example) will also test specifically for that aptitude. Inductive reasoning is about how you work through a problem systematically, not about your ability to express yourself visually.

 brilliant recap

Inductive tests use your reasoning skills to deduce which image fits into a sequence.

- You might have to predict which comes next in a sequence or identify which image fits earlier in a sequence.

● Using reason and logic you will puzzle out the rules which govern the way the images change in a sequence.

● You will also use creativity and flexibility when testing out whether your rules apply.

● All the information you need is there in the diagrams.

● You can make sense of the most baffling images if you look beyond the pictures to the underlying rules.

● Inductive, abstract and diagrammatic reasoning tests all measure the same ability.

8.5 How to tackle inductive reasoning tests

Working out the rules

Underlying every abstract reasoning test question are rules which govern how the shapes change one after the other. There may be only one or two rules at play, but they are rules which the shapes have to obey. You can also think of these rules as a relationship or pattern across the images. It would be unusual only to have one rule and generally you are looking for two or three rules, but it is only by working on the puzzle that you can be sure exactly how many rules are in play. Your task is to puzzle out these underlying rules because once you've sussed the rules which govern the question sequence, you apply those same rules to the answer options to identify the correct answer; there is only one correct answer. The level of complexity of these tests can vary, but you can use the same strategy regardless of how tricky they are.

The diagrams show you the rules

The diagrams you are given hold the answer you seek, because even in a short sequence of three diagrams, rules are being obeyed. These rules can relate to the objects within the diagrams, with predictable changes to: shading, position, size, number of sides, reflection or rotation of the objects. Does the change move clockwise from one image to the next, or maybe the changes move anticlockwise from one image to the next? Does an object change direction across compass points, moving say from north-east (NE) at top right to south-west (SW) at bottom left of the picture? Is there a pattern where the number of objects increases as you move across the sequence? This kind of pattern could just as easily be a decrease in the number of objects and the change in number might happen in every image in the sequence or in every other image in the sequence; checking across the whole sequence will reveal this.

The changes or differences can apply to the images consecutively, or to every other image, or be triggered by the inclusion of something distinctive within the image. Your task is to spot the patterns, so you can identify these rules and apply them in order to deduce which image logically comes next in the series.

 brilliant tip

Look for patterns and pay attention to the relationship between diagrams; the rules are there, before your very eyes.

The rules may follow principles of shapes and transformations
Remember that for this task you don't need any prior knowledge, because the clues you need to solve each puzzle are there, right before your very eyes. You need to read across the diagrams to see how they relate to each other: what remains the same, what changes? Having outlined some of the possible changes above, terms such as 'rotation' and 'reflection' might be familiar from maths you did at school (maybe even at primary school). This chapter will take you step by step through the reasoning process that you need for each practice question, but if you feel you need a more detailed explanation of these mathematical principles of shape, visit **bbc.co.uk/bitesize/ks3/maths/shape_space/**

Envisaging or deducing the correct answer

Ideally, if you manage to identify all of the rules, you should be able to form a picture of the missing image without even having to look at the answers you are given to choose from. However, given that your time is limited, it is a better strategy to eliminate systematically each answer that does not follow the rules as you identify them one by one.

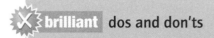 **dos and don'ts**

Do

✔ Look across the sequence of images for patterns and relationships.

✔ Expect there to be more than one rule in play.

✔ Look for increase, decrease, directional change, rotation, reflection and sequence.

✔ Eliminate answers systematically as you formulate each underlying rule.

Don't

✗ Forget to check the number of objects within each diagram.

8.6 Working through abstract reasoning tests one step at a time

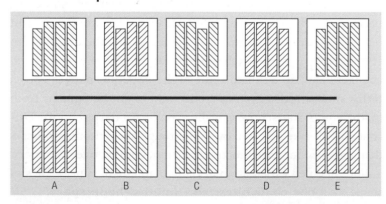

Identify what comes next in the sequence

Look at what features of the image could change

Your task is to identify patterns across this series of five images so you can determine what comes next in the sequence. Start off by looking for features of the images which could change: in this example, that could include:

- the number of bars;
- the heights of the bars;
- the position of the shorter bar(s);
- the direction of the stripes on the bars.

Focus your attention on one of these features

Pick one of these features, then look across the images to see if this changes, and if so, exactly how. Take the direction of the stripes in the bars – you can see straight away that the direction is not the same in all boxes. If you follow the sequence you can see that the direction alternates (it switches in the second box then switches back in the third box and then repeats this pattern) which gives you the first rule:

Identifying Rule 1

Rule 1: The direction of the lines on the bars alternates between going from top left to bottom right, then from top right to bottom left. Or, as expressed as points on a compass: NW–SE then NE–SW.

Applying Rule 1

Now you've got the first rule, you need to put it into practice so you can start to eliminate possible answers. Applying this rule you know that the stripes in the next box must be NE–SW, which leaves you with A, D or E as possible answers. So you need another rule to get down to the one correct answer.

Identifying Rule 2

Have a look at the heights of the bars – it is clear that the bars are not all the same size, and you can identify that there is always one bar in each box that is shorter than the others. However this is not enough to narrow down your answer options. Ask yourself what else changes? Notice the position of the shorter bar – it moves progressively to the right, which gives you:

> Rule 2: The shorter column moves one place to the right each time.

Applying Rule 2 to identify the correct answer

So the next in the sequence will have the shortest bar in the second bar position – which rules out options A and D, leaving you with the correct answer, E.

Let's try something that looks a bit different. But remember, the same principle applies – look across the images for patterns which identify rules, then apply them to find the correct answer.

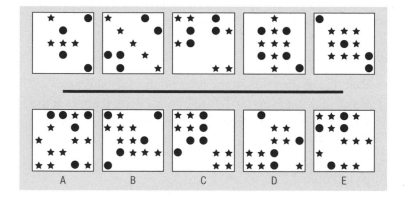

Identify what comes next in the sequence

Look at what features of the image could change

So what do we have here? There is a mixture of dark stars and circles. The features of the images that could change include:

- the number of stars;
- the number of circles;
- the position of the shapes in the box.

The more difficult abstract reasoning tests could involve a deeper level of pattern such as a relationship between the number of stars and the number of circles and how that might change.

Focus your attention on one of these features – the stars
If you consider these features you will note that the number of stars in the boxes changes. The number of stars, in order, is 4, 5, 6, 7, 8, which leads you to determine the first rule:

Identifying Rule 1

> Rule 1: The total number of stars in each box increases by one each time.

Applying Rule 1

Now you think you've got the first rule, try applying it. Which means you're looking for a box with 9 stars – this leaves you with answer options B and D.

Identifying Rule 2

You identified a pattern with the number of stars; so try the same with the number of circles. You'll notice that the number of circles changes in this order: 4, 5, 4, 5, 4, which gives:

> Rule 2: The total number of circles alternates between 4 and 5.

Applying Rule 2 to identify the correct answer

If the total number of circles next in the sequence should be 5, the correct answer is B.

Now you've worked through those examples, let's look at some slightly harder questions which involve more than two rules.

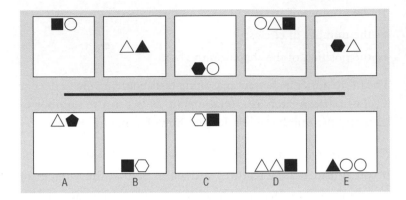

Identify what comes next in the sequence

Look at what features of the image could change

As before, start by looking at the images, thinking about the features present within those images and about how those features might change. Here the possible changes could be to: the number of shapes in the box; the shading of the shapes (whether just outline or shaded in black) and how that changes; the position of the shapes in the box (whether top, bottom or in the middle); and number of sides or edges of each of the shapes and how that changes.

Identifying Rule 1

Perhaps the clearest pattern to identify in this example is the position of the shapes moving from top to bottom. So:

> Rule 1: The group of shapes starts at the top of the box, moves to the middle, then to the bottom, then starts from the top again.

Applying Rule 1

Which means the one correct answer will have the shapes at the bottom. This leaves B, D and E as possible answers.

brilliant tip

> Notice where on the diagram shapes are positioned. If they
> move, track in which direction and remember things can move
> anticlockwise too.

Identifying Rule 2

When various shapes are involved it is often a good idea to consider the number of edges and the role that plays across the pattern. Remember that a circle doesn't have any sides, but does
have an edge – and that is what you are looking for. Counting
the total number of edges in each of the boxes in order gives: 5,
6, 7, 8, 9. Which gives you:

> Rule 2: the number of edges in each of the boxes increases
> by one each time.

brilliant tip

> Remember that a circle has an edge; include that if you are counting
> edges in a sequence.

Applying Rule 2

So you know the next box will need to have a total number of
sides of 10, which eliminates E and leaves you with two possible
answers, namely B and D.

brilliant tip

> When you identify a sequence of change notice whether that
> happens every single time, every other time or skips a time.

Identifying Rule 3

Now think about shading – in each box there is one shaded shape, so you know it's not the number of shaded shapes that changes. Before you get carried away in counting the number of edges, have a look at the position of the shape that is shaded, and you can identify:

Rule 3: The shading alternates between the first and last shape of each box.

Applying Rule 3 to identify the correct answer

Which means we're looking for an answer with the last shape shaded, which leaves only the correct answer, D.

 **tip**

It's best to apply each rule as you figure it out, so you narrow down the options and keep track of remaining possible answers.

Let's go through one more.

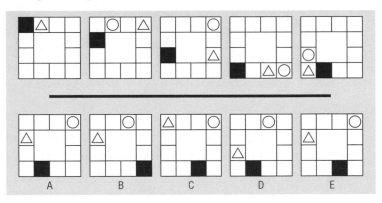

Identify what comes next in the sequence

Look at what features of the image could change

You can see that the position and number of squares in the grid around the edges of the boxes stay the same, so we don't need to pay that any more attention.

Focus your attention on the features that change

It is the circle, triangle and shaded square that move so you should take a moment to focus on these, trying to identify the pattern of their movement. Watch out for the circle in the very first image – it is almost hidden within the shaded square but you can see it.

Identifying Rule 1

Taking the circle first, tracking its movement across the images in the sequence you can establish:

> Rule 1: The circle moves clockwise, first one, then two, then three places as it progresses.

Applying Rule 1

So, imagining the circle moved on four places clockwise leaves you with A, C and E as possible answers.

brilliant tip

Don't assume that any movement will always be the same for each step. The rule in itself might be a pattern.

Identifying Rule 2

Now let's look at the triangle – this movement is regular, because each time it moves two places clockwise. Which gives us:

> Rule 2: The triangle moves clockwise two places.

Applying Rule 2

Applying this rule eliminates option C, but you are still left with two options that follow both of the rules you have established, so you'll need to determine a further rule which gets you to the correct answer.

Identifying Rule 3

Looking at the movement of the shaded square, you get:

Rule 3: The shaded square moves anticlockwise one place.

Applying Rule 3 to identify the correct answer

Which leaves you with the correct answer, E.

Strategies used in tackling these questions

Having worked through these questions and the reasoning behind the answers, you now have a handful of techniques which you can keep using to tackle any inductive/abstract/ diagrammatic reasoning test. Take a moment to reflect on how you got through the questions and see how many of the strategies you've already used just in this practice.

 **recap**

- You've looked at the diagrams carefully, trying to see if there is any pattern or relationship between the diagrams in the series.

- You've isolated the features that could change over the sequence.

- You've focussed on one changeable feature to start with, and have identified how it changes.

- You've noticed the sequence of the change – whether it is every single time, every other time or some other rule.

- You've noticed whether direction is involved in the change rule and whether that direction is across compass points, clockwise or anticlockwise.

- You've looked carefully at shading and orientation of shapes.

- You've noticed that sometimes the number of sides of shapes changes in a predictable way.

▶

- You've noticed that sometimes the number of edges of shapes changes in a predictable way.

- You've applied a rule as soon as you have identified it, so that you narrow down the answer options and keep track of what answers are still in contention.

- You've used logical thinking to puzzle out rules which you have applied.

- You've powered through to the one, correct answer.

8.7 Different tests and formats for this kind of reasoning

Just as there are different names for this kind of reasoning test (inductive, abstract, diagrammatic and logical) so there are variations in question format. Although the techniques you've used so far can be used in any of these kinds of tests, you need to know how the question formats can vary. There are also variations in the number of answer options and in the time limits per question.

Different formats in inductive/abstract/diagrammatic reasoning tests

Finding what comes next

The questions you have worked through above follow the most common format of abstract reasoning tests, where the instruction is to find what comes next.

Finding what is missing

One common variation you may come across is finding what is missing. This might be somewhere in a linear sequence or in a grid of images.

Finding what operates the sequence

Another variation is the 'operator' model: each question contains an input diagram, an output diagram and an 'operator' which affects how the image changes. Working on the patterns and relations between input and output leads you to identify the operator.

Preparing for test variations

It is worth checking with the employer what test format they use so it doesn't feel unfamiliar on assessment day. Regardless of question format or test label, you will need to demonstrate your abstract reasoning skills. So your best chance of success comes through practising on the 'what comes next' format, which will allow you to develop your reasoning. Try the next four questions on your own, using the techniques outlined above. Then read through the worked answers.

8.8 Practise your inductive reasoning

For each group of diagrams, identify what comes next in the sequence.

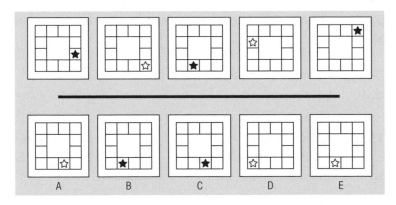

Q1 **What comes next in the sequence?**

(a) A

(b) B

(c) C

(d) D

(e) E

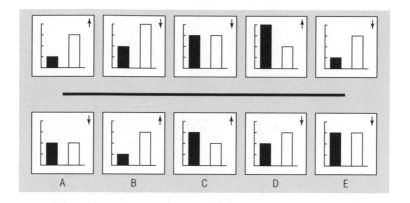

Q2 What comes next in the sequence?

(a) A

(b) B

(c) C

(d) D

(e) E

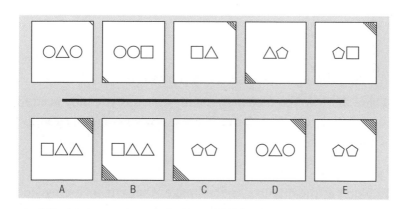

Q3 What comes next in the sequence?

(a) A

(b) B

(c) C

(d) D

(e) E

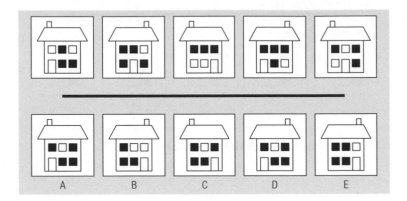

Q4 **What comes next in the sequence?**

(a) A

(b) B

(c) C

(d) D

(e) E

Working through the answers step by step

These first two questions are slightly easier as you only need to identify two rules in order to figure out what comes next in the sequence.

Features of Question 1

Looking at the features of the images that change across the sequence, you will notice that the star changes colour: sometimes it's block-shaded (a black star) and other times just outlined and blank in the middle (a white star). The star also changes position. Working through you will find that the following rules apply.

Identifying the rules

Rule 1: The star alternates between block-shaded (black) and outlined (white).

Rule 2: The star firstly moves clockwise 1 place, then 2 places, then 3 places and so on in sequence.

Applying the rules to identify the correct answer

Applying these rules means you are looking for an image with an outlined (white) star that has moved clockwise 5 places from the last image. This gives you the correct answer (e) E.

Question 2 – look at what features of the image change and how

Question 2 is a bit trickier. As always, start by noticing what are the features of the image. The heights of the two bars, the position of the shaded bar (there is always one bar shaded) and the direction of the arrow in the top right-hand corner.

Identifying the rules

It's fairly straightforward to identify the first rule.

Rule 1: The shaded bar increases one place each time, and when it reaches the top of the graph the pattern repeats from the beginning.

If you're struggling to identify a pattern, that probably means that you need to go deeper and identify relationships *between* the features. For example, does one feature changing in a certain way have an effect on the way another feature changes? In this case it's not clear what pattern the direction of the arrow follows, or the height of the unshaded bar. However, if you think about how these two features interact, one with the other, you can identify the second rule.

Rule 2: The arrow in the top right-hand corner determines whether the next unshaded block will move up or down one place.

Applying the rules to identify the correct answer

Eliminating answer options that do not follow these rules leads you to the correct answer: (a) A.

 **tip**

If you are struggling to identify a pattern you probably need to go deeper and look for a relationship between two of the changing features.

Features of Question 3

In working through this question you will find that there are 3 rules that you need in order to determine what comes next. Features include:

- how many notches there are in the corner;
- which corner the notches are in (top right or bottom left);
- how many shapes are in the box;
- what shapes are in the box and in what order; and
- the number of sides in the box.

Identifying the rules

Rule 1 governs the notches. Starting with the notches, which are the most obvious, brings us to formulate

Rule 1: The number of notches in the corner increases by one each time, and also the location alternates between top right and bottom left.

brilliant **tip**

Sometimes a rule is complex so has more than one part: if a rule doesn't work when applied, it might be too simple.

Rule 2 governs the number of shape edges. As the pattern for the shapes is not immediately obvious, it's worth having a look at the number of sides. This will give you:

Rule 2: The total number of shape edges increases by one each time. Remember that a circle has one edge so that's included in the count.

Rule 3 governs the shapes. Finally have a look at similarities between adjacent boxes. This gives you

Rule 3: The final shape in a box is the first shape of the next box.

Applying the rules to identify the correct answer
Applying these three rules leads to the correct answer, which is (b) B.

Features of Question 4

Don't let the fact that the image is recognisable deter you from the fact that it is just made up of different features that change. These features include: the number and position of shaded 'windows', the position of the 'door' and the position of the 'chimney'.

---

brilliant tip

If the diagram is recognisable as a picture, keep looking for the features which change, even if they too are depicting something familiar. Identify patterns, not pictures.

Identifying the rules
Looking carefully, you can identify:

Rule 1: The chimney alternates between the left and right-hand side of the roof.

Rule 2: The door moves one place to the right each time and when it reaches the end, the pattern repeats again from the start, following the same rule.

As the position of the shaded windows do not seem to follow a clear pattern, try counting the number of shaded windows. This identifies:

Rule 3: The number of shaded windows alternates between 3 and 4.

Applying the rules to identify the correct answer
Applying all three of these rules leaves the correct answer: (e) E.

 practice

Now check that you understand what inductive reasoning is asking you to do by trying the Chapter 8 practice inductive test in Part 3, Brilliant practice. Check that you are using the brilliant tips here as strategies for tackling inductive reasoning tests.

---

brilliant dos and don'ts

Do

✔ Identify the features in the images that change – this will be your basis for establishing the rules.

✔ Eliminate answer options as you identify rules to keep.

✔ Keep track of remaining possible correct answers.

Don't

✗ Be thrown by an image that you recognise (e.g. a house, a flower etc.) – focus on the features that make up the image, which can change over the series.

▶

✗ Forget that a change in number of a feature is not always
   consecutive – it may be alternating or increase/decrease by one
   more each time (e.g. move 1 place, then 2 places, then 3...).

✗ Overlook the fact that sometimes the features of an image
   interact with each other.

✗ Waste time considering features of an image that don't change
   across the sequence.

✗ Panic if you can't immediately see a pattern; focus on just one
   feature and track it across the series to see whether it changes.

CHAPTER 9

Situational judgement tests

⏶ **brilliant** learning

By the end of this chapter you will:

1 understand what the questions in situational judgement tests (SJTs) are asking you to do

2 have a clear strategy to minimise your stress and maximise your performance in SJTs.

9.1 What do situational judgements actually test?

Situational judgement tests are designed to test how you work through a situation, choose a course of action and then implement it. An important underlying test is that you recognise that any chosen course of action (in a given situation) is likely to have some kind of consequence. Additionally, they test whether you appreciate there is more than one way to tackle a situation, but that some ways are more effective than others.

So before you even set foot on the employer's premises, SJTs give an insight into how you work, how you could adapt to a new role, how you make and implement decisions which directly affect colleagues, staff and ultimately the business or organisation in which you are employed. This can help an employer build up a fuller picture of you as a candidate, over and above what an application form can tell.

The situations depicted in SJTs are common across pretty much every type of organisation and indeed any sector of work. They frequently look at working in a team as this is extremely common in a workplace, irrespective of exactly what the business is. The ability not only to lead a team but to understand the dynamics of effective teams is highly prized. Note that the SJT asks you to work out what you would do in a hypothetical situation; it doesn't ask you to present something from your own direct experience. So even if your experience in the workplace is limited, you can still work through the situations and demonstrate your judgement of situations.

'SJTs are not at all technical. They're about pressures and judgements and team-working and doing the right thing. No prior knowledge is needed and no work experience is needed.'

Sara Reading, Royal Bank of Scotland

In common with all the other psychometrics we're discussing in this book the SJT is carefully designed for its purpose – which is to measure judgement as a basis for comparison across applicants.

 **brilliant** definition

Situational judgement tests
Situational judgement tests are carefully designed to probe how you weigh up options and decide what actions to take so as to resolve work-based problems.

9.2 What does a situational judgement test look like?

SJTs are all written out, which makes for a lot of reading. Typically, the SJT starts by outlining the job role you are to imagine yourself doing – trainee hotel manager or civil servant, for example. You are then given a situation. Sticking with the examples just given, it could be that you are duty manager for the day, or that you have to brief a minister before a public meeting. Next follows a series of situations, again relating back to that job role in that situation – someone asks you to give them a discounted room rate, or the local news reports warn of feelings running high in advance of the public meeting. You'll then be given a range of possible responses to that situation; four answer options is typical. At this point you'll be asked to apply your judgement of the situation. It is worth noting that there are a couple of variations in terms of what you are instructed to do at this point.

'If there are a lot of questions (especially similar questions) it's quite easy to lose focus, especially when there's not necessarily a right answer and you can't just guess.'

Hannah, BSc Economics and Politics

Choosing one answer

Having put yourself into the role and thought through both the situation and the possible responses, you then apply your judgement. You might be asked to choose just one of the possible responses, either the one you think would be most effective or the action that you would be most likely to perform.

Putting all the answers in rank order

You might be asked not to choose just one but to rank all four in order, either from most to least effective action or from what you personally would be most likely down to least likely to perform.

Rating each answer on a five-point scale

You may be asked to comment on all the answer options, rating each on a five-point scale for either effectiveness or personal style. You've probably weighed them all up, one against the other, in order to choose one; this answer style simply requires that you show that thinking process.

Of course it is important that you pay attention to the instructions so you understand how your answer is to be presented. But no matter what form the answering takes, your judgement of the situation is what is under scrutiny and you can tackle all the various formats in exactly the same way.

 **recap**

> Check the instructions: are you looking for the most effective course of action, or the action you would be most likely to take? Are you instructed to choose just one answer, or to rank all of the answers in order?

Some variations

Filmed scenarios

A slight variation on the written SJT is where tests are administered online. This opens up the possibility of using films or film clips. This approach can also be used at an assessment centre, where you would be doing the test at a dedicated computer. Although the medium varies, the underlying test remains the same: how you judge a situation and how you then choose what action to take. The answer format is the same too – you would be presented with a number of possible actions that could be taken, and invited either to choose one or rank them all according to the instructions.

brilliant tip

> Although you might find variations in the way you present your answers, you tackle all situational judgement tests in the same way.

The in-tray exercise

An in-tray exercise challenges you to work through a sequence of tasks by simulating a typical (if rather eventful) working day. Often you start on the first task given, only to find other demands are made of you. You are also likely to get updates as you are working; a new complication or competing pressure. The in-tray exercise can be done online or in person at a test centre. It is unlikely that you will be given a range of answers to choose from; you have to tackle the tasks and juggle the competing demands according to your judgement.

9.3 What does a situational judgement test feel like?

In contrast to the reasoning tests (verbal, non-verbal and diagrammatic), the situational judgement test can sometimes feel less challenging. You're not doing the obvious cognitive tasks associated with reasoning like calculation and analysis, but you are being tested just as much on your thinking and you need to be alert to that demand. With so much to read and the answers often being only subtly different from each other, you need to be aware that your attention can drift; keep focussing on the task before you.

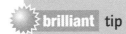 **tip**

SJTs are designed to test your thinking and how you make judgements; be aware of that and focus on the task before you.

9.4 How to tackle a situational judgement test

Read the instructions

The instructions are not complicated, but you do need to be clear about the task you are undertaking. You might be asked to choose one of the answers on offer – either the most effective action to take, or the action you yourself would be most likely to take. You might be asked to choose two of the answers on offer – the most and the least effective actions to take, or the most and least likely action you yourself would take. Or you might be asked to rank all the answer options in order, from most to least effective or from most to least likely you would take.

brilliant tip

Pay attention to the instructions: do you choose one or rank all of the answers? Are you judging what would be most effective or what you would be most likely to do?

Read the scenario

Read the scenario and put yourself in the situation described. Really picture yourself doing that particular job as that situation starts to unfold. By doing this you will take on the role and the responsibilities of that role, which should help you to start thinking along the right lines. Don't worry about never having had the actual experience described; the SJT is simply asking you to think about the possible options you can choose from if you were in that job. Don't dismiss the situation or the role out of hand as being not the kind of thing you want to do; stay with the situation and work through it. Finally, don't relax because you've actually had a similar experience in the workplace; pay attention to what is presented to you as this scenario and these possible actions. Of course you will bring your experience into it, but bear in mind what the job itself would require, and the underlying values of the employer.

brilliant tip

You don't have to have had direct experience of the job role in the scenario; just put yourself in those shoes and go ahead as if you were in the job.

Read all the answers through before answering

Read through each and every answer before choosing one option. If you dismiss the first one you read, or latch on to the first one you read, you might miss something important in the others. Don't jump to conclusions; use your situational judgement.

Answering as instructed

Check that you understand how you are expected to answer the question. It could be choosing one answer, choosing two answers, ranking all possible answers in order or rating all possible answers. Check also that you have understood what you are choosing: the most effective action or the action you would be most likely to perform.

 **recap**

> Later in this chapter there will be an example which is worked
> through for you. Then you'll try a practice question on your own,
> and, again, you'll be taken step by step through the working out.
> Finally, you'll do a whole test on your own, in your own time.
> Answers will be provided!

Is there a right answer?

In contrast to all the reasoning tests, there is not one correct answer to the SJT questions. There is, however, one answer which the test is looking for. That is the course of action which works most effectively, according to the company's values. Companies and organisations are very open about their values, because they want to attract employees who will work with their ethos and culture. You can readily locate this information on their promotional literature and or their websites. It may be listed under different headings, such as core values, competencies, mission statement or vision.

'With SJTs, it's important to research the company. The Civil Service outlined all the key competencies they were looking for; it's just useful to have in the back of your mind, especially when you're in doubt over which answer to choose.'

Hannah, BSc Economics and Politics

Whose values come into play?

There is a delicate balance to be struck when you are asked to choose what would be the most effective answer. The balance is between what your natural instinct might be and what the company is likely to consider the most effective course of action. You can suppress your personal preference and skew your answers so they reflect the company. In the short term, that might seem like a smart move, because it could lead to you landing the job. There is a danger in the longer term, however, which is that you might end up being offered a job which ultimately isn't 'you'. The smart thing to do is to treat the SJTs as a window into the company's soul; look at it closely to get a sense of whether you'd feel comfortable doing this job in this company.

 'A big thing about the SJT is self-selection – helping people to decide. We might not be as aggressive a department as they want to work in or they might think it's too fluffy. Or it might totally resonate and they might think it's absolutely right for them.'

Sara Reading, Royal Bank of Scotland

Managing your time in SJTs

The time allocated for completing these tests doesn't put you under the same pressure as when the clock counts down during online verbal and numerical reasoning tests; in some cases there may be no time limit at all. If you are doing this online then it might be entirely up to you how long you take. You'll need to read the various situations and weigh up the answer options, so you will need to manage your own time effectively, finding a balance between speed and attention. With practice, you'll find a good pace in which you pay attention but keep moving on through the questions. There is a danger in over-thinking which leaves you confused and off-balance. Generally speaking, you'll find that your first answer is probably the one to go for.

9.5 How to tackle an in-tray exercise

There are two main options for where you would take an in-tray exercise: either online or on site. If it is on site that would either be at the employer's premises or alternatively at an assessment centre. If online, then you'd most probably take it in the comfort of your own home or maybe in a library or some other place where you can get internet and computer access. Either way, you will be expected to complete the whole in-tray exercise within a specified period of time.

It can help to sketch out a to-do list that you can refer back to and amend as the situation emerges. Don't waste time on making this elaborate – it should just help you to focus on the key tasks in hand. There isn't necessarily one right way, but there are behaviours and actions which are more effective and therefore more sought after by the selectors.

brilliant tip

Writing a to-do list can help you to focus and prioritise the in-tray exercise. Remember it's only one tool – do it roughly and then get on with the tasks facing you.

When you identify a highly pressurised scenario, be aware that you can consider delegating some tasks, and/or asking for help from colleagues or indeed from your line manager. Don't get too carried away with delegation; you need to give a clear indication of what actions you yourself would take to recover the situation.

Managing your time during an in-tray exercise

Time is also an issue in the 'in-tray' exercises, but also keeping your head when more and more things are landing on your desk or in your inbox. A more generous time allowance brings its own challenges too: the Civil Service Fast Stream 'in-tray' exercise takes two and a half hours – of your online time. So you'll need to make sure you are comfortable before you start; while there is nothing stopping you wandering off to make yourself a drink or take a comfort break, that's time lost from tackling the exercise.

brilliant dos and don'ts

Do

✔ Have a look at what employers say about their values and the competencies they are looking for.

✔ Check whether to choose or rank your answers.

✔ Imagine yourself doing the role described.

Don't

✘ Latch on to or dismiss any one answer until you have considered them all.

✘ Panic if you've never had experience in the role.

✘ Over-think your answers; trust your instinctive choice.

9.6 Working through situational judgement tests one step at a time

Practice situational judgement test

Scenario 1:

You are a manager at the Saldringham branch of a national DIY superstore chain. The chain is called Distinctly DIY and you are one of four duty managers who work daily shifts at the Saldringham store and who report to the Store Manager.

The store is divided into two main areas:

1   interior DIY, plumbing and decorating

2   exterior DIY, gardening, garden buildings and furniture.

There are usually two duty managers working on any one shift and each duty manager will be responsible for one of the two areas. The shifts are 7.30am to 3.30pm and 12.30pm to 8.30pm. The store is open 8am to 8pm every day apart from Sundays when it is open from 10am to 4pm. The duty manager is responsible for managing staff, overseeing stock control and dealing with any difficult complaints or queries. There are eight full-time shift team leaders who report to the duty managers and act as shopfloor supervisors whilst also serving customers.

When a fellow duty manager is on annual or sick leave then the other duty manager and the Store Manager share responsibility for managing their half of the store.

There are 84 staff employed at your branch in total, on both a part-time and a full-time basis.

Situation 1:

You have arrived for work at 7.30am on a Friday to find that, out of the 19 staff due in for the early shift on the 'exterior DIY and gardening' area, five have not turned up. You are responsible for this area today.

▶

All five of the absent staff have caught a severe flu-like virus which is affecting a high number of people in Saldringham at the moment. Today is due to be very busy as you are expecting a large delivery of garden sheds and Fridays are often quite busy in the shop as people pop in to stock up on DIY and gardening supplies for the weekend. The gardening team leader and the exterior DIY team leader inform you that to unload the delivery and deal with the store customers effectively this morning they need a minimum team of 17 people.

Review the following responses A to D and indicate which one you believe to be the response to the situation you would be 'most likely to make' and the response to the situation which you would be 'least likely to make'.

Responses:

(A) Delegate the problem to the team leaders to sort out.

(B) Tell the team leaders to engage three agency staff today to deal with the delivery and other outstanding tasks.

(C) Call a staff meeting and tell all staff to make sure they get an inoculation against the virus.

(D) Call all members of the part-time Saturday staff team and ask whether they can come in today for a few hours.

Read the first scenario, the situation and the answer instructions

The instructions are to review all four responses and rate them from the response you, personally, would be 'most likely to make' down to 'least likely'. Each response must be considered in turn. The answers worked here can't assume knowledge of you personally, so are considered from the employer's perspective of what is most effective.

Rating each response in turn

Response A suggests delegating the problem. But the situation is both urgent and important; staff are absent, sales are important and you are responsible. Sorting this should be your top priority so delegating it is not a particularly appropriate response.

Response B suggests getting agency staff in. This will help with getting key tasks done, but will incur cost – although that could be offset by securing sales for the day. Also, agency staff will need to be briefed if they are new to the store. This is a reasonably effective response.

Response C suggests telling staff to get inoculated against the virus. This does nothing to address the immediate situation so is the least effective response.

Response D is to call in Saturday staff to work extra hours today. This solves the staff absence, ensures work will be covered, incurs some costs but is efficient because staff will know what they need to do. It is, therefore, the most effective response. So the rating from 'most likely to make' to 'least likely' would be: D, B, A, C. Let's try another.

Scenario 2:

You are currently employed as an operational manager for UK Airports plc. You are based at Saldringham airport which is a small but growing airport serving primarily domestic destinations but which has recently added a selection of international routes, mainly to popular holiday destinations. The airport serves approximately 2 million passengers per year. You work on rotation as duty manager. Your responsibilities as duty manager are to ensure the smooth running of the airport, including passenger services, commercial operations, security and airside services.

Situation 2:

You have just been having an informal catch-up with the Airside Security Team Leader, Simon Bryant. He informed you during your conversation that one of his team, Graham Cooper, a Senior Security

▶

Officer, has taken a rather high number of sick days over the last few months. In fact, Graham's sickness absence for the last three months is much higher (ten days) than it was a year ago for the same period (two days).

Simon said to you that the sick days have mostly been one day here or there, with no significant long run of absence. Simon has followed the correct procedures by having a chat with Graham upon his return from each absence to check that everything is OK; however, Simon hasn't been able to work out if there is a serious medical issue or if something else is going on for Graham. Simon has never had to deal with a case like this before as he is new to the role of team leader. UK Airports plc have a formal interview procedure which a manager must conduct with a staff member if they are absent for more than two days in a month. Clearly this is now the case for Graham; however Simon is a little anxious about running this process, due to his relative inexperience.

Review the following responses A to D and indicate whether you believe the response to be 1 – The most effective response 2 – The second most effective response 3 – The third most effective response or 4 – The least effective response. You may assign each rating only once.

Responses:
- (A) Offer to sit in with Simon when he conducts the meeting and give him feedback afterwards.
- (B) Suggest that you conduct the meeting and Simon can take notes.
- (C) Book in some time very soon to talk through the process of running the sickness absence interview with Simon and ensure he is confident with the task.
- (D) Give Simon details of the link on the UK Airports plc internal website which gives full information about the sickness absence management procedure.

Read the second situation and the answer instructions

The instructions are to review all four responses and rank them from most to least effective. You have a forced choice here in that you can only use each rating once and once only.

Rating each response in turn

Response A is to sit in with Simon. This could be of use but doesn't help him develop understanding of the process or what approach he could take in the meeting. Not the most effective response.

Response B is that you conduct the meeting. Simon learns nothing by this and his position is undermined. The least effective response.

Response C is to make time to take Simon through company procedures so he knows what to do. This develops his capacity and ensures due process. The most effective response.

Response D is to refer Simon to the company website. This is even less effective than A, because it doesn't help Simon move forward with the task or his ability to undertake it.

You can probably fix C as the most effective and B as the least effective, but might have to think about the order for A and D. Don't fall into the trap of over-thinking; with the top and bottom fixed, go with your first instinct in how to order these two. This is where judgement comes in and practice will help with that. So the ranking from most to least effective is: C, A, D, B.

Scenario 3:

You are the manager of a distribution depot for SuperSwift Deliveries. SuperSwift provides clients with a timely courier and distribution service for dry goods of any volume or weight.

▶

The company has a chain of depots throughout the UK and a fleet of large volume lorries for moving goods large distances around the country. Each depot also has a number of smaller collection and delivery vans. These vans are used for local distribution of goods once they have been sorted and prioritised for delivery at the depot. They are also used to collect goods from customers to sort for outbound distribution to other parts of the country.

You manage 52 depot processing staff who work in three shifts (each shift has a shift manager) to sort the goods that arrive from other depots and from local customers. You also have a team of 36 collection and delivery drivers who report to a delivery team manager who reports into you. The lorry drivers, who bring goods into the depot from elsewhere in the country and who collect goods for national distribution, are managed centrally from SuperSwift HQ and are not your direct managerial responsibility.

The depot is open 24 hours a day, 364 days a year.

Situation 3.

It is 8am on a Monday and you have arrived at work to find an urgent note from your assistant on your desk. She says that Ms Beverly Thornton, SuperSwift Director of Operations, has called to say she is on her way for a 'drop in' visit this morning. She will be arriving at about 10.30am and hoping to have a chat with you and some of your depot staff just to see how everything is going. She would also like to see your last quarter's service quality figures and details of any ongoing customer issues. You have never met Beverly before as she is a recent addition onto the SuperSwift Board of Directors.

Review the following responses A to D and indicate which you believe to be the 'most effective' response to the situation and which the 'least effective'.

▶

Responses:

(A) Let Beverly 'take you as she finds you' and do little more than your usual morning routine until she arrives. Let the team know she will be visiting. Ask your assistant to sort out the figures and information that Beverly has asked to see.

(B) Inform the team that Beverly Thornton is visiting this morning and tell them who she is. Ask your assistant to sort out the figures and information that Beverly has asked to see. Review the SuperSwift company report to remind yourself of Beverly's background and career and to make a guess at her likely areas of interest.

(C) Call an emergency meeting of the depot processing shift staff and the drivers who are not out on the road. State that they must put on a 'good display' for Beverly as she is a very senior manager and there might be implications for the depot if she takes a poor view.

(D) Do nothing apart from your usual work; you are confident that Beverly will be impressed with what she finds in your depot.

Read the third scenario, the situation and the answer instructions

Your task is to identify the most and the least effective response to the situation from the four options. Is there anything in the scenario which gives you a sense of the company's values? Having done that, you can work your way through each of the possible actions, considering to what extent they would be effective in this scenario.

Working through each response in turn

Response A suggests minimal action in preparation for this important visitor. Sounds reasonable.

Response B is comprehensive, inclusive (you tell the team) and ensures you get some sense of what your visitor might want to focus on. Sounds pretty effective.

Response C doesn't prepare you, doesn't secure the data she wants and could be upsetting. Not at all effective.

Response D doesn't upset anyone, but doesn't get the data your visitor wants. Not effective.

Working through each response in turn identifies B as the most and C as the least effective. You don't need to pay any further attention to A and D because you've now done what the question wanted.

Scenario 4:

You are a manager of a product advisory team in Dunlow & Farnham (D&F), a company that provides financial services to private customers in the UK. D&F have a broad range of products such as mortgages, savings accounts, secured loans and personal loans.

Your team of advisors are responsible for advising customers and potential customers on which D&F product is right for them; they have sales targets which vary from product to product. Your team deals with customers across the East Midlands region of England (This encompasses the combined area of Derbyshire, Leicestershire Rutland, Northamptonshire, Nottinghamshire and most of Lincolnshire).

D&F do not have high street branches so advisors meet customers in their homes or talk to them over the phone. Most of your advisors work from home and are located across the region. The East Midlands region is very large and it is advantageous to have a geographical spread of advisors working across the area.

Situation 4:

You have a new advisor who has just joined the team and taken over the Rutland and North Leicestershire patch from Bob Prindiville. Her name is Nikki Patel, she has attended a three-week headquarters induction and product training course and it is her first week 'on

▶

patch' this week .You went out on appointments with her yesterday to provide support where necessary and she seemed reasonably competent and confident. She has called you this morning to ask whether you can help her with a customer request that she has had. She is due to meet the customer this afternoon and he wants her advice on the right loan for his daughter who has just left university and wants to buy a car. The customer is willing to guarantee the loan for his daughter.

Review the following responses A to E and indicate whether you believe the response to be 'very effective', 'effective', 'slightly effective', 'ineffective' or 'counterproductive'. You may assign each rating only once.

Responses:

(A) Talk through the details of the customer's requirements and situation with Nikki. Find out what the loan amount is, what the daughter's income is likely to be and how long they want the term of the loan to be. Choose a product based on this information.

(B) Look at your team's sales for the last month and suggest the most popular loan product based on those data.

(C) Suggest the 3 Year Fixed-Interest Loan as your team hasn't sold many of those this quarter and is falling short of target.

(D) Suggest the 'Responsible-Guarantor Loan' which D&F launched 2 years ago. It allows someone to guarantee a loan for someone else in case they should default on the payments.

(E) Gather as much information as you can from Nikki about the customer and his daughter. Suggest one or two options and explain your reasoning to Nikki.

Read the fourth scenario, the situation and the answer instructions

Your task is to rate the four possible responses to the situation from very effective down to ineffective and beyond, to counterproductive. Is there anything in the scenario which gives you a sense of the company's values? There is reference to sales targets, but also to advising customers on products that are right for them. Your new advisor seems competent, but needs your help.

Working through each response in turn
Response A includes systematic consideration of the key variables involved in offering a loan, working through the facts. This is an effective response.

Response B does take account of the sales targets set, but does not take into account what is known about the customer's needs. An ineffective response therefore.

Response C focuses on sales, and to some extent on the team's needs, but completely sidelines any consideration of the customer. Worse than ineffective, this response is counterproductive.

Response D could be the right product, but makes some assumptions and doesn't take into account all the key facts needed. A slightly effective response.

Response E covers all the bases. You are working with everything you know about the customer's needs at this point, along with everything you know about the range of products your new sales advisor has to offer. By taking her through your own thinking in whittling down the choices, you are educating her both in the products on offer and how that could fit with what a customer really wants, once you get more detailed information. A very effective response.

You have to use all five categories, but you can only use them once. It can help to fix one, then calibrate the other answers in relation to that fixed point. It is probably easiest to fix the counterproductive one then work up to the most effective. You can always re-jig the order; the key thing is to make a start somewhere.

9.7 Strategies used in tackling these questions

Having worked through the questions and the reasoning behind
the answers, you now have a handful of techniques which you can
keep using to tackle any situational judgement test. Take a moment
to reflect on how you got through the questions and see how many
of the strategies you've already used just in this first practice.

 **brilliant** recap

Take a moment to reflect on how many of these strategies you used
in the example questions:

- You've understood whether you are choosing an effective course
  of action, or the action you would be likely to perform.

- You've understood whether you are choosing one answer or
  ranking all of the answers in the order required.

- You've taken on the role depicted, put yourself in the frame and
  taken decisions as if you were in that job.

- You've read through all the answer options, giving each one
  due consideration before making your decisions.

- When you've been torn between two answers, you've gone with
  your first instinct and moved on to the next challenge.

- You were aware that this is a test of your thinking and judging.

- You stayed focussed on the task throughout.

brilliant practice

Now check that you understand what situational judgement tests are asking
you to do by trying the Chapter 9 practice situational judgement test in
Part 3, Brilliant practice. Check that you are using the brilliant tips here as
strategies for tackling verbal reasoning tests.

One last word from an employer before you head off to practise:

 'With the situational judgement test, we don't want to focus on the competencies, it's got to be about the values. It's about your instinct and your judgement and how those align to our values.'

Sara Reading, Royal Bank of Scotland

CHAPTER 10

Personality tests or indicators

By the end of this chapter you will understand what personality tests are asking you to do and be clear about how to tackle them.

10.1 What do personality tests actually measure?

In common with other psychometrics, personality tests are used to measure the mind. Whereas all the reasoning tests (whether verbal, numerical or diagrammatic) and the situational judgement tests are measuring aptitude and ability, personality tests are assessing your personal qualities. These qualities range far and wide, encompassing traits which would very clearly sit within an employment context (such as motivation and drive), along with traits which are equally relevant to work (such as values and interests) and all the personality traits which sit at the heart of what makes you the unique individual that you are.

What kind of personality traits are there?

Given the complexity of the human mind, there are numerous personal qualities which can be examined. Most of the personality tests commonly used for selection focus on a handful of dimensions. You may see reference to The Big 5 or OCEAN, which is the acronym for openness to experience, conscientiousness, extraversion, agreeableness and neuroticism. You don't need any level of detail about these in order to take a personality test but they can be broadly depicted as follows: openness to experience includes creativity and imagination or a thirst for knowledge; conscientiousness embraces diligence, efficiency, being steadfast and thorough and working hard; agreeableness is the ability to get on with other people and to show kindness; extraversion finds enjoyment in company and can be impulsive; and finally neuroticism is being prone to anxiety and depression.

brilliant definition

Psychological tests

'There are two main types of psychological test. Those that measure aptitudes/ability or attainment and those designed to assess personal qualities such as personality, beliefs, values, interests, motivation or drive.'

British Psychological Society

Is there a right answer?

In all the reasoning tests, you are set a problem to which there is only one correct answer; your task is to work that out. With the situational judgement tests there is also one preferred answer – usually the one that is most effective in moving the situation forward in line with the organisation's values and mission. With personality tests, there is no right or wrong answer. It's a measure of the mind and it's all about you.

Is there a personality type which is right?

Of course, if it were only all about you, employers wouldn't have any reason to use personality tests as part of their selection and recruitment processes. They use them to gain a fuller picture of you as a job applicant, alongside other instruments such as the aptitude and ability tests, the application form, the interview and group tasks. When taken as part of that whole, personality traits can be more or less desirable in different job roles. Of course, someone who is by nature more introverted may well be capable of acting in an extravert way if the job demands it, but they won't necessarily feel at ease when doing so for a sustained length of time. Role profiling, when used appropriately, can enable an individual to play to his or her strengths.

'We use personality questionnaires to see what type of person they are. How high they score on pragmatist and extravert relates to how well they do in the customer service centre.'

Sim Sekhon, Managing Director, Legal4Landlords

10.2 It really is all about you

Even though you are taking this test because an employer requires you to do so as part of their application process, ultimately a personality test is all about you. There's no calculating or working out demanding your attention; it is a concentrated focus on who you really are. This can reveal new aspects or confirm what you already know. Either way, taking a personality test can enrich your knowledge and understanding of what you are.

'For any candidate applying, self-knowledge is key; you've got to know yourself – your strengths, your weaknesses. If you don't know yourself, you're lost.'

Oliver Wheedon, Business Analyst

You, just the way you are

There is no point trying to cheat a personality indicator. For a start, these tests are carefully constructed according to scientific protocol so maintaining a false position isn't straightforward. More importantly though, if you were to give answers that don't really reflect your personality, all you are doing is pretending to be someone you're not. It may be that, as the selection process unfolds, you begin to have second thoughts about the job you are applying for. Pay attention if that happens to you – it may not sound likely, but getting into a job that really isn't for you is not such a great outcome. There are other jobs, other possibilities, which will allow you to be authentic and revel in your unique set of values and strengths.

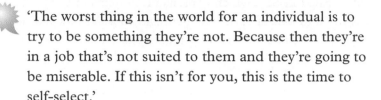

'The worst thing in the world for an individual is to try to be something they're not. Because then they're in a job that's not suited to them and they're going to be miserable. If this isn't for you, this is the time to self-select.'

Sara Reading, Royal Bank of Scotland

10.3 What does a psychometric test look like?

You'll be presented with a series of written questions or statements. Tests vary in length from around 20 items to more than 60 items. In some cases the same test can be taken in either a long or a short version. Duration therefore varies too, from as little as 15 up to 60 minutes or more. It is only in very specific tests that you'd be given any images to interpret, so you can expect to read through a series of questions or statements.

'Most questions are actually straightforward and not trying to trip you up. I wasted a lot of time at the beginning looking for the tricks, when the best way is to go with your first instinct.'

Devika, BSc Philosophy, Politics and Economics

What's the answer format?

There are really only two answer formats. You might be invited to agree with one of several statements. Or you might be invited to rate how much you agree with each statement, estimating to what extent it describes you or sounds like you. When doing a test online you simply click on your chosen answer. When doing a test on paper, you tick or shade in your chosen answer.

Example questions

Try these questions, taken from the Transferable Employability Skills Scale (TESS), which consists of 19 items in total.* You are invited to look at each statement and consider how true it is for you, then circle the answer you have chosen.

'I know what I can do well'

Not at all	Slightly	More or less	Very	Entirely
true	true	true	true	true

'I normally speak up when there's a problem'

Not at all	Slightly	More or less	Very	Entirely
true	true	true	true	true

'I don't find it easy to get people to do what I want'

Not at all	Slightly	More or less	Very	Entirely
true	true	true	true	true

You may have noticed that the third question is phrased negatively; this happens routinely in tests and just means you might have to read it twice to be sure you are clear on its meaning. This is one way of keeping you focussed on the test.

More example questions

Here's another clutch of questions, this time taken from a pilot psychometric for entrepreneurial potential which comprised 70 items.** You are invited to look at each statement and rate to what extent that statement describes you, then circle the answer you have chosen.

'I don't blame others for the way things turn out'

Does this describe you:

Not at all	Poorly	More or less	Very well	Entirely

---

* This scale was developed by Professor Rachel Mulvey in 2011.
** This prototype scale was developed by Professor Rachel Mulvey in 2013.

'I really want to make decisions about how my life is'

Does this describe you:

Not at all   Poorly   More or less   Very well   Entirely

'I'm in charge of how my life turns out'

Does this describe you:

Not at all   Poorly   More or less   Very well   Entirely

'My success doesn't depend on others'

Does this describe you:

Not at all   Poorly   More or less   Very well   Entirely

You may have noticed that all these questions look like they are probing the same kind of issue. In the original pilot, they weren't presented one after the other but interspersed among all 70 questions. With longer questionnaires in particular, there may be a number of rather similar questions which appear throughout the test. This is part of the test design, in order to give careful consideration to differing facets of the same aspect of personality. The challenge for you is to maintain your concentration and carefully read the question which is actually in front of you.

'If there are a lot of questions (especially similar questions) it's quite easy to lose focus.'

Hannah, BSc Economics and Politics

10.4 What do psychometric tests feel like?

In contrast to the effort demanded by the reasoning tests, taking a personality test can feel rather relaxing. You might also find that you are genuinely curious to see what the test reveals about you to yourself. You're certainly not under pressure to work out the right answer, and you don't have the pressure of a timer counting down while you're working; both of these may come as a welcome relief.

However, you may find it hard to keep focussed on the test simply because it doesn't explicitly demand the same mental workout as all the reasoning tests. Equally, you may feel anxious, worried that you have to match up to an ideal personality type. You might also find yourself stuck on a question because you can't quite see yourself in that situation; it can help in this case to think of what you would do in a work situation and answer from that perspective. Ultimately, personality tests do feel different from aptitude tests because they are different. So the best tactic is to stay alert and give yourself up to the test, confident that by doing so you will probably enhance your self-knowledge.

 **brilliant** practice

Now check that you understand what personality tests are asking you to do by doing an online test at **assessmentday.co.uk**

 **brilliant** recap

- Doing a personality test gives you valuable self-knowledge.
- Relax – the questions are not designed to trip you up.
- Stay true to yourself and give authentic answers.
- If in doubt, assume the questions want a work context response.
- Stay alert, particularly if you sense there is some repetition.
- Don't agonise – there really isn't a right answer here.

Brilliant
practice

Chapter 1 What are psychometric tests?

The brilliant learning from Chapter 1 was that you would *understand five different types of tests which are commonly used by employers*. Check your understanding of what are the most common psychometric tests used by employers by taking this true/false quiz. The answers are in Part 4, Brilliant answers.

For each of the following statements, decide whether it is true or false.

1.1 **If an employer uses psychometric tests as part of the recruitment process they will use the whole range of tests available.**

True   False

1.2 **Verbal reasoning tests only look at your understanding of the passage you have to read.**

True   False

1.3 **You will come across the same kind of reasoning tests whether the employer is in public or private sector and even across engineering and banking.**

True   False

1.4 **Either you get reasoning or you don't – practising won't help.**

True   False

1.5 **Situational judgement tests measure skills like problem-solving and team-working, which can transfer across employer and sector.**

True   False

1.6 **Personality tests can give you a real insight into the kind of person you are so can be useful if you don't get the job in telling you something about whether that job would have suited you.**

True   False

1.7 Psychometrics are the best way of selecting for a job.

True   (False)

1.8 You can't really do a situational judgement test unless you've already worked in that role.

True   (False)

1.9 Public and private sector use the same reasoning tests.

(True)   False

1.10 Personality tests help you check whether the job is really right for you.

(True)   False

Chapter 2 Why do employers use psychometric tests?

The brilliant learning from Chapter 2 was firstly that you would *understand why employers use psychometric tests for selection and talent management* and secondly that you would *know how psychometric tests are used alongside other selection techniques*. Check your understanding of why employers use psychometric tests by taking this true/false quiz.

The answers are in Part 4, Brilliant answers.

For each of the following statements, decide which is true and which is false.

2.1 Employers use psychometrics so as to get the best person for the job.

(True   False

2.2 Psychometrics indicate that if you're good in the test you'll be good in the job.

(True)   False

2.3 Employers like to reject people and use tests as an excuse to do just that.

True   ~~False~~

2.4 They just make these quizzes up; they can put anything down and call it a test.

True   False

2.5 The only time you'll have to do a psychometric test is to get started in your career.

~~True~~   False

2.6 Employers use psychometrics alongside other selection methods such as interview.

True   False

2.7 You've got to get a much higher score than just the benchmark on every test.

True   False

2.8 Doing a great application is more important than passing an online test.

True   False

2.9 Employers sometimes sequence tests; you have to pass one to get access to the next.

True   False

2.10 Thinking about how you got on helps you make sense of career decisions.

True   False

Chapter 3 What to expect and how to prepare for tests

The brilliant learning from Chapter 3 was firstly that you would *understand how preparing for tests can help you* and secondly that you would *be able to adopt a mindset which minimises nerves and maximises your performance.* Check your understanding by reading these four scenarios and choosing which action you would be most likely to take.

The answers are in Part 4, Brilliant answers.

3.1 **The online tests for the FabGrad mega-scheme close at the end of November.**

Do you:

(a) Set aside the 28 November and work out a day by day test preparation schedule for the next 12 weeks.

(b) Factor in a couple of practice sessions and a test date, working around other commitments.

(c) Relax – November is miles away.

3.2 **It's mid-November, your laptop is acting weird and so is everyone in your house.**

Do you:

(a) Put a notice up on the fridge telling them of your issues and splurge money on a new PC.

(b) Look into booking a private study space and reserving a computer for last week of November.

(c) Reckon that weird is the new normal, and that everything will ˅ sort itself out.

3.3 **You log on to the FabGrad website, start the clock and can't answer anything.**

Do you:

(a) Sob hysterically.

(b) Breathe out and focus.

(c) Chillax.

3.4 **You somehow get through the FabGrad online test and immediately you:**

(a) Ask everyone you know who did it to share their answers and working out with you.

(b) Take half an hour to work out what was OK and what needs a bit more practice.

(c) Move on to something more interesting.

Chapter 4 What if I don't get through?

The brilliant learning from Chapter 4 was that you would *identify how to use your experience of psychometric tests for personal and professional development*. There are two tasks you need to undertake for this test.

Task 1 – Use an online career planning tool

You can choose either the skills health check offered by the National Careers Service or the career planner offered by Prospects. Please note that Prospects is designed for graduates so if you are studying for a degree (either foundation, honours or masters) or have recently graduated, Prospects is the one to try.
www.nationalcareersservice.direct.gov.uk/tools/ skillshealthcheck
www.prospects.ac.uk/myprospects

Task 2 - Reflective learning (allow at least 15 minutes; paper and pen needed)

Start by locating a recent experience of doing a psychometric test. Focus on your experience of that situation: how did you feel? What was going through your mind? How did you react? What did you do? What was the feeling after the action was completed? Remember that positive feelings are just as important, so pay attention to those too. The challenge is to zoom in on you, in your world, as you experienced this event.

Next, consider whether you would you do anything differently if you found yourself in a similar situation in the future. Would you change your actions? Your behaviours? Your reactions? The way you felt? If everything went well and there is nothing you would change, that's ok; just remember what it was that worked for you so you can draw on that again in the future.

Finally, identify what exactly you would do differently. Commit to this change in future action.

Chapter 6   Verbal reasoning tests

The brilliant learning from Chapter 6 was that you would *understand what the questions in verbal reasoning tests are asking you to do* and that you would *have a clear strategy to minimise your stress and maximise your performance*. Try this set of six tests, on your own, within the time limit set (25 minutes). The answers are in Part 4, Brilliant answers.

Founded in 1954, the Bilderberg Group holds an annual conference of 120 of the world's most powerful and influential people. Participants, invited by a steering committee comprised of two people from each of 18 different countries, typically include financiers, industrialists, politicians, royalty and newspaper editors. Past delegates have included

▶

Tony Blair and Bill Clinton, shortly before becoming heads of state. Reporters, however, are not invited: the Bilderberg Group's meetings are conducted in privacy, with strict confidentiality rules to foster open discussion. The Group was established to promote understanding and cooperation between the United States and Europe and to create an informal network for the global elite. No votes are taken at the conference and no policies are agreed. However, the secrecy surrounding the conferences has given rise to numerous conspiracy theories. Right-wing critics believe that the Bilderberg Group is a shadowy global government, with some conspiracy theorists holding the Group responsible for organising events including the overthrow of Margaret Thatcher, the Bosnian War and the invasion of Iraq. Left-wing activists, who call for greater transparency, accuse the Group of being an unelected capitalist cabal controlling world finance. While opponents view the Group as undemocratic, supporters argue that modern democracies depend on cooperation between banking and politics, and that organisations such as the Bilderberg Group help ensure their success.

Q1 **The Bilderberg Group has critics on both sides of the ideological spectrum.**

True   False   Cannot say

Q2 **Representatives from the media are not allowed to attend the Bilderberg Group conference.**

True   False   Cannot say

Q3 **The Bilderberg Group was created as a private forum to set Europe and America's political and financial agenda.**

True   False   Cannot say

Q4 **Topics discussed at Bilderberg Group conferences have included the invasion of Iraq.**

True   False   Cannot say

Q5 **Because its delegates are not elected, the Bilderberg Group's activities are widely believed to be undemocratic.**

True   False   Cannot say

▶

Although today used to describe any movement to claim back territory for ethnic, linguistic, geographical or historical reasons, the term irredentism originally came from the Italian nationalist movement Italia irredenta. Meaning 'unredeemed Italy', Italian irredentism was an opinion movement rather than a formal organisation. It sought to unify ethnically Italian territories, such as Trieste, Trentina, and Istria, that were outside of Italian borders at the time of the unification of Italy in 1866. The annexation of these Italian territories from Austria provided Italy with its strongest motive for participating in World War I. The Treaty of Versailles in 1919 satisfied most of Italy's irredentist claims, however new borders delineated by the treaty gave rise to new irredentist claims. Dividing the German Empire into separate nations created German minority populations in the new countries of Poland and Hungary. German irredentist claims to these territories, as well as to Austria, resulted in the Second World War. The Treaty of Versailles created Yugoslavia to be a Slavic homeland, but ethnic and religious differences between Bosnians, Serbs and Croats eventually led to war in the 1990s. The artificial political states created by the Treaty of Versailles in East Africa failed to take tribal boundaries into account, and thus remain subject to irredentist claims. Similarly, borders drawn up in the Near East are still contentious today.

Q6 **Trieste, Trentina and Istria were reunified with Italy following the Treaty of Versailles.**

True	False	Cannot say

Q7 **Borders imposed in 1919 by the Treaty of Versailles resulted in twentieth century conflicts.**

True	False	Cannot say

Q8 **Irredentist movements advocate the annexation of territories only on the grounds of prior historical possession.**

True	False	Cannot say

▶

Q9 Yugoslavia was created following the Second World War to provide a homeland for Bosnians, Serbs and Croats.

True   False   Cannot say

Q10 Although originally an Italian movement, irredentist claims are now being made in other countries.

True   False   Cannot say

Many organisations predict that the global water crisis presents this century's biggest threat. Today 84% of people in developing countries have access to clean water, 2 billion more than in 1990. However, millions still lack clean water for drinking and sanitation, posing a major health threat. In the developed world, water consumption is unsustainably high, doubling every twenty years. Agriculture accounts for 70% of the world's fresh water use, and an increasing population to feed means this demand will only increase. Groundwater sources, used to irrigate crops, are running dry because of overuse. While limiting the use of groundwater is a possible solution, it would have a financial impact on farmers and result in lower yields. While climate change has resulted in increased precipitation in some areas, it is contributing to water shortages in other regions. Rising temperatures have caused the Himalayan glaciers, the source for all of Asia's major rivers, to retreat. A reservoir for nearly half of the world's fresh water, these glaciers are predicted to lose four-fifths of their area by 2040. The solution to the global water crisis lies predominantly in new technologies. Desalination plants, which convert seawater into fresh water, have now been built in countries including Israel and Singapore. The process's high costs however limit its widespread adoption. Organising bodies and treaties are also needed to ensure that cross-border water sources are managed properly and do not become a source of conflict.

▶

Q11 The global water crisis has resulted in less of the world's population having access to fresh water.

True   False   Cannot say

Q12 The irrigation of crops comprises the majority of groundwater usage.

True   False   Cannot say

Q13 Despite increasing rainfall in some areas, climate change is the main cause of the global water crisis.

True   False   Cannot say

Q14 The main impediment to desalination is expense.

True   False   Cannot say

Q15 Both technological innovation and diplomacy are needed to tackle the world's water crisis.

True   False   Cannot say

Esperanto is an artificial language constructed in 1887 by the eye specialist Dr Ludovic Zamenhof. Having experienced ethnic divisions and language barriers growing up in Poland, he aimed to create an easy-to-learn second language that could transcend cultural and political differences and further international peace.

Although Zamenhof's goal of a universal auxiliary language was not realised, today there are 1.6 million Esperanto speakers in more than 90 different countries. Using an alphabet comprised of five vowels and 23 consonants, Esperanto is based on Indo-European languages. Its grammar has logical rules with no irregular verbs, and its spellings are phonetic, making Esperanto about five times easier for a native English speaker to learn than French or Spanish. While some Esperanto speakers still advocate the adoption of the language

▶

worldwide, other proponents see its value primarily as a language-teaching tool. Esperanto is on the curriculum in countries including China and Hungary, but it is not taught in British schools because it lacks an associated culture. Its lack of culture is a common criticism levied at Esperanto, yet its neutrality was intended to foster equality between speakers. Detractors also argue that Esperanto's linguistic roots give an unfair advantage to speakers of European languages. The newer constructed language Loglan is based on logic and uses the world's six most widely spoken languages – Arabic, Mandarin, English, Hindi, Russian and Spanish – as its vocabulary's source.

Q16 **One of the advantages of Esperanto is that it is universally easy to learn.**

                          True   False   Cannot say

Q17 **Dr Zamenhof's goal was to replace ethnic languages with the universal language of Esperanto.**

                          True   False   Cannot say

Q18 **Esperanto's lack of an associated culture or homeland can be viewed as both an asset and a disadvantage.**

                          True   False   Cannot say

Q19 **Contemporary Esperanto speakers do not share a common vision of the language's purpose.**

                          True   False   Cannot say

Q20 **Loglan is a more logically constructed language than Esperanto.**

                          True   False   Cannot say

A study has estimated that 20% of Americans have used prescription drugs for non-medical reasons, while the number of deaths from accidental drug poisoning has quintupled since 1990. Prescription drug abuse is the fastest-growing drug problem in the United States and most experts concur that the cause is the increased availability of powerful new opioid analgesics. When taken as prescribed, opioids are a safe, effective form of pain management with an addiction rate of only one percent. The rise of pain clinics and online pharmacies, however, has made it easy for non-medical users to procure these potent painkillers. The family medicine cabinet is another common source of opioids, as well as sedatives and stimulants, which young people often combine with other drugs and alcohol. Despite many highly-publicised deaths from prescription drug abuse, there persists a popular misconception that using prescription medicines without a prescription is legal, safe, and less addictive than taking recreational drugs. While education programmes for youths and healthcare providers are being introduced to raise awareness of prescription drug abuse, there are calls for increased government regulation over opioid dispensation. Measures such as patient tracking and urine testing could help doctors identify addicts.

Some healthcare professionals have expressed concern that restricting opioids in such ways would have an adverse effect on chronic pain sufferers who rely on such medications. Until the pharmaceutical industry develops less lucrative but non-addictive painkillers, there are few alternatives to opioids for treating chronic pain.

Q21 **Prescription drug abusers are typically young adults who have access to the drugs at home.**

> True   False   Cannot say

Q22 **The pharmaceutical industry has made opioid painkillers highly addictive to enhance their profits.**

> True   False   Cannot say

Q23 **Prescription drug abuse in the United States is generally attributed to the availability of strong opioids.**

> True   False   Cannot say

▶

Q24 The erroneous belief that there are fewer risks associated with taking prescription drugs recreationally is prevalent.

True   False   Cannot say

Q25 Medical professionals do not support proposed government restrictions on the prescription of opioids.

True   False   Cannot say

Birds were long considered stupid, however laboratory research has shown that corvids – the group of birds including crows and jays – are actually highly intelligent. Their ability to make and use tools rivals that of chimpanzees. When hiding stores of food, corvids demonstrate their episodic memory and future planning ability – cognitive abilities previously thought unique to humans. Not only do corvids remember where they have caught food, they remember when they stored it. If seen catching food, corvids will return and re-hide it, unobserved by competitors. This anticipation of pilfering shows that corvids acknowledge the mental state of other individuals. Being the most social group of birds, corvids raise their young cooperatively and form long-term relationships. The social function of intellect theory, which hypothesised that social living was the impetus for the development of primate intelligence, is now applied to other species, such as corvids. Although capable of doing many of the same things as primates, corvids have smaller brains and lack the neocortex that is responsible for mammalian cognition. Instead, corvids have a nidopallium, which scientists believe fulfils a similar function more efficiently. Primate and corvid intelligence is sometimes used as an example of convergent evolution, whereby two unrelated species independently develop the same adaptations to similar environmental conditions. But animal intelligence is a controversial subject, with no consensus on its definition. Some

▶

scientists argue that corvid behaviour can be explained by adaptive specialisation and is not equivalent to primate intelligence, and thus convergent evolution does not apply.

Q26 **Corvids' feeding behaviour indicates that they have some awareness of what their competitors are thinking.**

                         True   False   Cannot say

Q27 **The social function of intellect theory states that corvid intelligence developed as a result of their complex social structure.**

                         True   False   Cannot say

Q28 **Although they lack a common ancestor, primates and corvids acquired their intelligence under the same evolutionary processes.**

                         True   False   Cannot say

Q29 **Corvids' cognitive abilities are the result of both brain structure and social structure.**

                         True   False   Cannot say

Q30 **A corvid's nidopallium is smaller, but more powerful, than a primate's neocortex.**

                         True   False   Cannot say

Reproduced with permission from www.assessmentday.co.uk

Chapter 7 Numerical/non-verbal reasoning

The brilliant learning from Chapter 7 was that *you would understand what the questions in non-verbal/numerical reasoning tests are asking you to do* and that you *would have a clear plan of attack to minimise your stress and maximise your performance.* Try this test, on your own, within the time limit set (30 minutes). The answers are in Part 4, Brilliant answers.

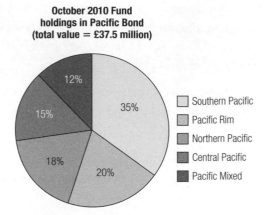

October 2010 Fund
holdings in Pacific Bond
(total value = £37.5 million)

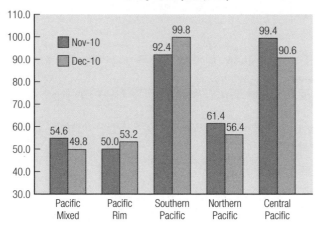

Monthly Value (£100,000s)

Q1 **What was the 2010 percentage change in the value of the Pacific Rim holding between October and November (to the nearest percent)?**

(a) 41% less

(b) 41% more

(c) 36% less

(d) 34% less

(e) 33% less

Q2 **What was the ratio of Pacific Rim: Southern Pacific holdings in October 2010?**

(a) 3:2

(b) 2:3

(c) 4:5

(d) 5:4

(e) 4:7

Q3 **In October 2010 which two Pacific Bond fund holdings when combined had the same value as Southern Pacific holdings?**

(a) Northern Pacific and Central Pacific

(b) Central Pacific and Pacific Rim

(c) Pacific Mixed and Pacific Rim

(d) Pacific Mixed and Northern Pacific

(e) Pacific Rim and Northern Pacific

Q4 **Which of the following represents the largest amount?**

(a) October's Pacific Mixed holding

(b) Average November value of each of the 5 holdings

(c) November value of holdings in Northern Pacific

(d) 70% of November's value of holdings in Southern Pacific

(e) Average December value of each of the 5 holdings

Q5 **In October 2010 what fraction of the total Pacific Bond did the Northern Pacific and Pacific Mixed fund holdings represent?**

(a) 1 / 5

(b) 1 / 10

(c) 1 / 4

(d) 3 / 10

(e) 2 / 5

Western Region – Store location	Number of sales staff	Units sold					
		Week 1		Week 2		Week 3	
		Actual	Target	Actual	Target	Actual	Target
Redcliff	8	20	15	20	25	35	35
Ather	9	30	20	40	25	40	35
Wilkington	5	25	20	18	25	24	30
Trew	8	15	10	14	15	12	15
Tunston	6	5	10	6	15	9	15

Q6 **For Weeks 1 and 3, across all 5 stores combined, what was the difference (in units) between Actual and Target sales volumes?**

(a) 10 over target (Week 1); 10 under target (Week 3)

(b) 10 over target (Week 1); 15 under target (Week 3)

(c) 15 over target (Week 1); 10 under target (Week 3)

(d) 15 over target (Week 1); 15 under target (Week 3)

(e) 20 over target (Week 1); 10 under target (Week 3)

Q7 **Over the three week period, which store achieved the highest sales per sales staff member?**

(a) Redcliff

(b) Ather

(c) Wilkington

(d) Trew

(e) Tunston

Q8 Next year, staff numbers are to be reduced by 1 at stores
with 6 or fewer staff, and by 2 staff at all other stores. What
will be the average monthly target per staff member across
all 5 stores if the regional target (across the 5 stores) is
£168,000?

(a) £5,000

(b) £6,000

(c) £7,000

(d) £8,000

(e) £9,000

Q9 The Western region's overall sales (£120,000) were in a
ratio of 3:2 to the Eastern region's sales which itself had half
the sales of the Northern and Southern regions combined.
What were the total sales of all 4 regions?

(a) £180,000

(b) £200,000

(c) £220,000

(d) £240,000

(e) £360,000

Q10 All sales in the three week period were based on an
average £9.50 reduction in the sales price of the units sold.
What was the total saving made by customers who bought
units over the 3 week period (to the nearest £100)?

(a) £3,000

(b) £3,500

(c) £4,000

(d) £4,500

(e) £5,000

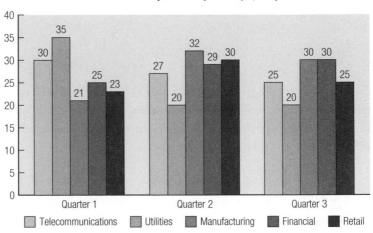

Consultancy income by sector (£1,000s)

Manufacturing sector – Consultancy income by consultant

Consultant	Quarter 1	Quarter 2	Quarter 3	Quarter 4
David	4,000	3,500	5,000	4,000
Peter	6,000	6,500	7,000	10,500
Sarah	6,000	9,000	5,500	3,000
Jane	4,000	4,500	7,500	4,500
Harry	1,000	4,500	5,000	6,500

Q11 **Which sector experienced the highest sales for Quarters 1, 2 and 3 combined?**

(a) Telecommunications

(b) Utilities

(c) Manufacturing

(d) Financial

(e) Retail

Q12 **Quarter 4's income per sector is in the same ratio as Quarter 3, and the consultancy income from the Financial sector is £33,000. What is the consultancy income from the Utilities sector?**

(a) Can't tell from the data provided

(b) £12,000

(c) £22,000

(d) £25,000

(e) £45,000

Q13 **For Quarters 1 and 3 combined, which two Manufacturing sector consultants had incomes in the ratio 2:3?**

(a) Harry and David

(b) Sarah and Jane

(c) Harry and Jane

(d) David and Peter

(e) David and Sarah

Q14 The Manufacturing sector income from the five consultants is supplemented by the work of an associate consultant. What was the associate consultant's income from the Manufacturing sector across Quarters 1 to 3?

(a) £3,000

(b) £4,000

(c) £6,000

(d) £8,000

(e) £9,000

Q15 The total quarterly income target, starting with £115,000 for Quarter 1, increased by 20% for each subsequent quarter. In Quarter 3 what was the difference between actual income and the target?

(a) £8,000 under-performance

(b) £18,400 under-performance

(c) £31,000 over-performance

(d) £31,000 under-performance

(e) £35,600 under-performance

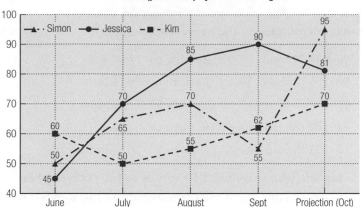

Client visits (per month) by 3 Sales Managers

Q16 **Simon and Jessica have travel allowances of 60p and 44p per mile respectively. Simon and Jessica each travel on average 25 miles and 30 miles respectively per sales visit. How much travel allowance is claimed in total by these two sales managers in August?**

(a) £1,050

(b) £1,122

(c) £2,122

(d) £2,172

Q17 **If the percentage change in sales visits between September and October (projected) continues for November, what will Jessica and Kim's number of complete sales visits be in November?**

(a) 71 visits (Jessica); 77 visits (Kim)

(b) 71 visits (Jessica); 78 visits (Kim)

(c) 72 visits (Jessica); 78 visits (Kim)

(d) 72 visits (Jessica); 79 visits (Kim)

(e) 73 visits (Jessica); 79 visits (Kim)

Q18 **If the margin of error on October's projected client visits is +/− 15%, what are the ranges for each sales manager (rounded to the nearest whole visit)?**

(a) 90-100 (Simon); 77–85 (Jessica); 66–74 (Kim)

(b) 90–107 (Simon); 74–87 (Jessica); 64–76 (Kim)

(c) 81–109 (Simon); 73–89 (Jessica); 63–77 (Kim)

(d) 81–109 (Simon); 69–93 (Jessica); 60–81 (Kim)

(e) 76–104 (Simon); 64–89 (Jessica); 56–76 (Kim)

Q19 **Jessica, who travelled 3,500 miles in July, travelled an extra 10 miles per client visit compared to Simon. What was the total number of miles Simon travelled in July?**

(a) 2,400

(b) 2,600

(c) 2,800

(d) 3,000

(e) 3,200

Q20 **The average order values per client visit are £145, £135 and £125 for Simon, Jessica and Kim respectively. Which sales managers generated the highest and lowest order values in June?**

(a) Kim (most); Jessica (least)

(b) Simon (most); Jessica (least)

(c) Jessica (most); Kim (least)

(d) Jessica (most); Simon (least)

(e) Kim (most); Simon (least)

US operations Year 1	Subsidiary 1	Subsidiary 2	Subsidiary 3	Subsidiary 4	Subsidiary 5
Sales*	1,124	3,334	2,250	24,300	14,450
Salary payroll for all staff	127	409	289	570	4,355
Number of staff	555	1,722	1,343	2,824	13,292
Dividends per share (cents):					
1. Interim dividend paid	6.2	8.5	9	15	11
2. Final proposed dividend	15.8	10.5	46	10	25
Number of shares (millions)	3	3.5	12	2.6	20

*in $100,000s

Q21 Which subsidiary will pay the lowest amount in dividends (interim and final dividends combined)?

(a) Subsidiary 1

(b) Subsidiary 2

(c) Subsidiary 3

(d) Subsidiary 4

(e) Subsidiary 5

Q22 Which 2 or 3 subsidiaries had combined sales of 1,890.8 million?

(a) Subsidiaries 1 and 5

(b) Subsidiaries 2 and 5

(c) Subsidiaries 1, 2 and 5

(d) Subsidiaries 3 and 5

(e) Subsidiaries 1, 3 and 5

Q23 **Over the next year, Subsidiary 5's sales are expected to drop by a fifth whilst its number of staff is expected to increase by 15%. What will be the percentage change in the sales per member of staff from Year 1 to the next?**

(a) 25%

(b) 26%

(c) 29%

(d) 30%

(e) 44%

Q24 **What is the ratio of Subsidiary 4's interim dividend per share compared to Subsidiary 5's final dividend per share?**

(a) 2:3

(b) 5:2

(c) 2:5

(d) 3:5

(e) 5:3

Q25 **What is the lowest payroll per member of staff (across the 5 subsidiaries)?**

(a) £23,751

(b) £22,883

(c) £21,519

(d) £20,764

(e) £20,184

Consolidated Income Statements (£millions)	Competitor A	Competitor B	Competitor C
Revenue	580	632	600
Gross profit	128	148	147
Operational profit	108	128	131
Profit before tax	90	112	117
Corporation tax*	−27	−33.6	−35.1
Profit after tax	63	78.4	81.9

*Tax = 30%

Q26 **If Profit before tax increases by 15% for Competitor B and decreases by 8% for Competitor A, what is the difference between Competitor A and Competitor B's corporation tax payments (to the nearest £million)?**

(a) £10 million

(b) £12 million

(c) £14 million

(d) £16 million

(e) £18 million

Q27 **Competitor B and Competitor C choose to declare their Revenues in US dollars ($) and Euros (€) respectively. What are these figures? (Use the exchange rates £1 = $1.66; £1 = €1.15).**

(a) $1,043 million (Competitor B); €708 million (Competitor C)

(b) $1,049 million (Competitor B); €690 million (Competitor C)

(c) $1,049 million (Competitor B); €720 million (Competitor C)

(d) $720 million (Competitor B); €1,055 million (Competitor C)

(e) Can't tell from the data provided

Q28 What would be the difference in Euros if Competitor A used an exchange rate of £1 = €1.20, rather than £1 = €1.15, when calculating its profit after tax?

(a) €0.05 million

(b) €1.15 million

(c) €2.05 million

(d) €3.05 million

(e) €3.15 million

Q29 What was the average gross profit across the 3 competitors (to the nearest £10 million)?

(a) £140 million

(b) £141 million

(c) £142 million

(d) £143 million

(e) £144 million

Q30 Competitor C moves to a country charging 15% corporation tax and corporation tax falls to 22% for Competitors A and B. What is the total corporation tax payable for the 3 competitors (based upon the profit before tax figures shown)?

(a) £62 million

(b) £46 million

(c) £26 million

(d) £25 million

(e) Can't tell from data

Reproduced by permission from www.assessmentday.co.uk

Chapter 8 Inductive, abstract and diagrammatic reasoning

The brilliant learning from Chapter 8 was that you *would under-stand what the questions in inductive, abstract and diagrammatic reasoning tests are asking you to do* and that *you would have a clear plan of attack to minimise your stress and maximise your per-formance.* Try this test, on your own, within the time limit set (25 minutes). The answers are in Part 4, Brilliant answers.

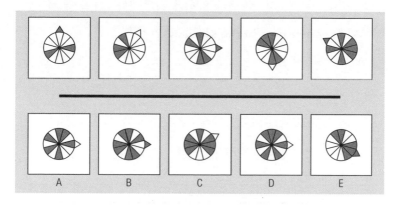

Q1 **What comes next in the sequence?**

(a) A   (b) B   (c) C   (d) D   (e) E

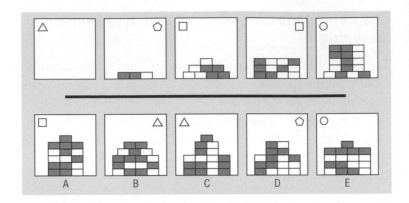

Q2 **What comes next in the sequence?**

(a) A   (b) B   (c) C   (d) D   (e) E

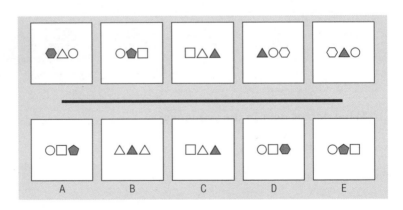

Q3 **What comes next in the sequence?**

(a) A   (b) B   (c) C   (d) D   (e) E

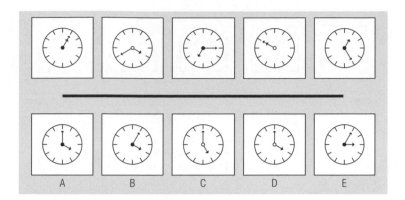

Q4 What comes next in the sequence?

(a) A   (b) B   (c) C   (d) D   (e) E

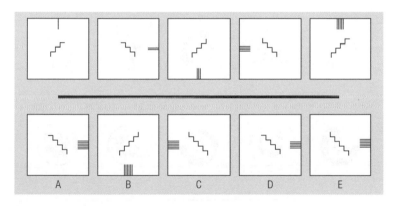

Q5 What comes next in the sequence?

(a) A   (b) B   (c) C   (d) D   (e) E

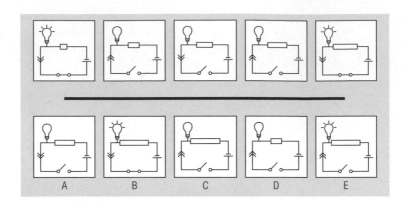

Q6 What comes next in the sequence?

(a) A   (b) B   (c) C   (d) D   (e) E

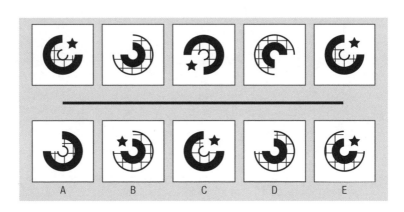

Q7 What comes next in the sequence?

(a) A   (b) B   (c) C   (d) D   (e) E

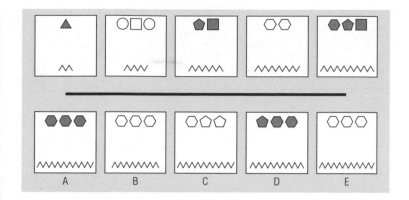

Q8 What comes next in the sequence?

(a) A   (b) B   (c) C   (d) D   (e) E

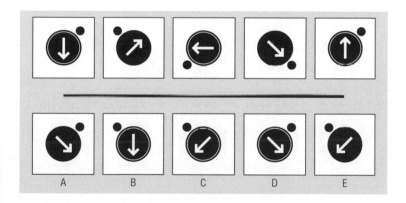

Q9 What comes next in the sequence?

(a) A   (b) B   (c) C   (d) D   (e) E

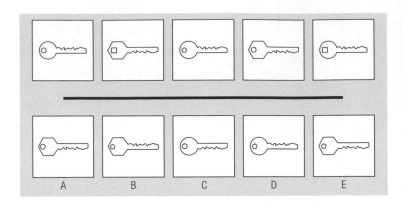

Q10 What comes next in the sequence?

(a) A   (b) B   (c) C   (d) D   (e) E

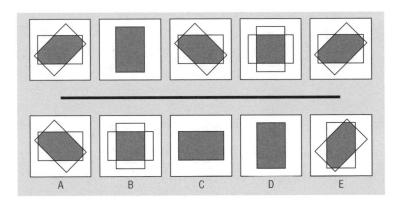

Q11 What comes next in the sequence?

(a) A   (b) B   (c) C   (d) D   (e) E

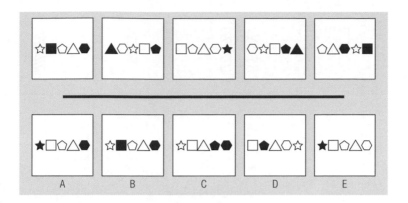

Q12 What comes next in the sequence?

(a) A   (b) B   (c) C   (d) D   (e) E

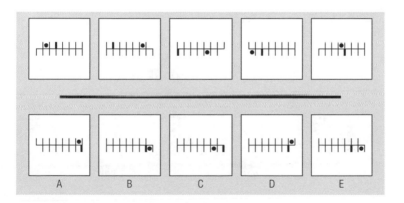

Q13 What comes next in the sequence?

(a) A   (b) B   (c) C   (d) D   (e) E

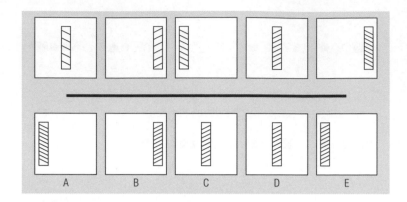

Q14 **What comes next in the sequence?**

(a) A   (b) B   (c) C   (d) D   (e) E

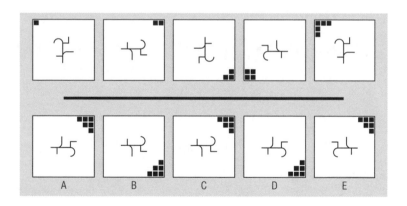

Q15 **What comes next in the sequence?**

(a) A   (b) B   (c) C   (d) D   (e) E

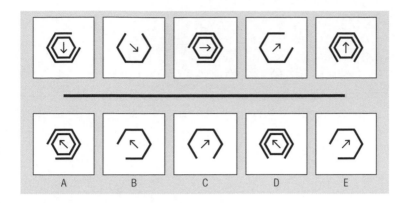

Q16 What comes next in the sequence?

(a) A   (b) B   (c) C   (d) D   (e) E

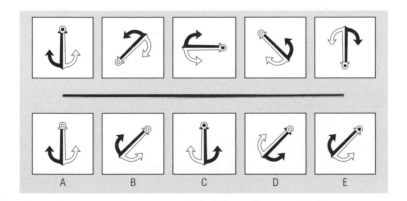

Q17 What comes next in the sequence?

(a) A   (b) B   (c) C   (d) D   (e) E

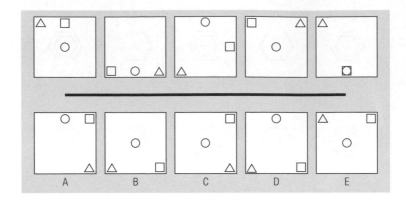

Q18 **What comes next in the sequence?**

(a) A   (b) B   (c) C   (d) D   (e) E

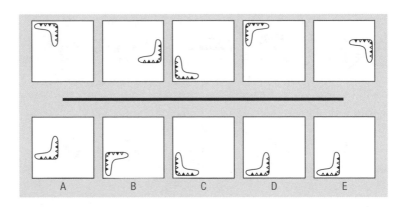

Q19 **What comes next in the sequence?**

(a) A   (b) B   (c) C   (d) D   (e) E

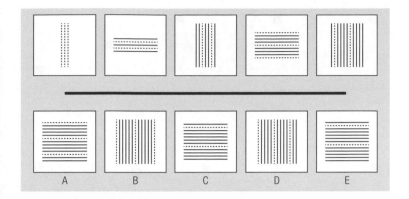

Q20 What comes next in the sequence?

(a) A   (b) B   (c) C   (d) D   (e) E

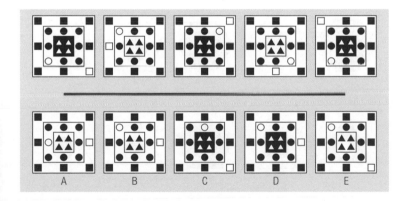

Q21 What comes next in the sequence?

(a) A   (b) B   (c) C   (d) D   (e) E

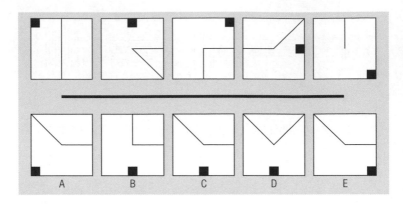

Q22 **What comes next in the sequence?**

(a) A   (b) B   (c) C   (d) D   (e) E

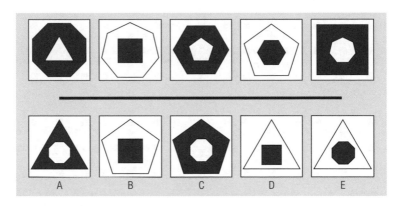

Q23 **What comes next in the sequence?**

(a) A   (b) B   (c) C   (d) D   (e) E

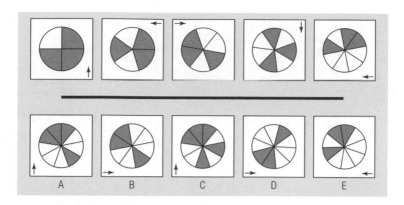

Q24 **What comes next in the sequence?**

(a) A   (b) B   (c) C   (d) D   (e) E

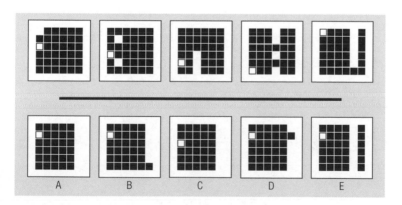

Q25 **What comes next in the sequence?**

(a) A   (b) B   (c) C   (d) D   (e) E

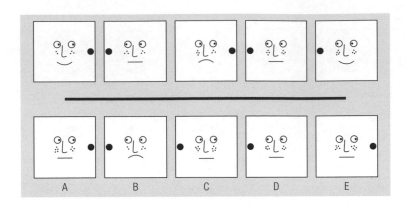

Q26 What comes next in the sequence?

(a) A   (b) B   (c) C   (d) D   (e) E

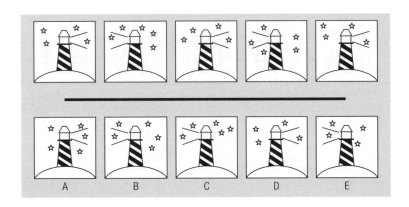

Q27 What comes next in the sequence?

(a) A   (b) B   (c) C   (d) D   (e) E

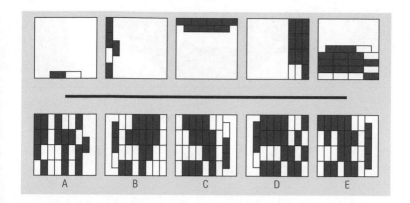

Q28 **What comes next in the sequence?**

(a) A   (b) B   (c) C   (d) D   (e) E

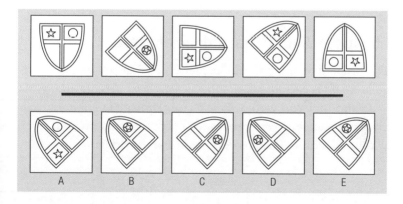

Q29 **What comes next in the sequence?**

(a) A   (b) B   (c) C   (d) D   (e) E

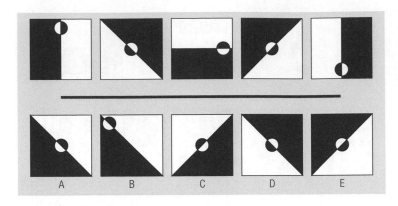

Q30 **What comes next in the sequence?**

(a) A   (b) B   (c) C   (d) D   (e) E

Reproduced with permission from www.assessmentday.co.uk

Chapter 9 Situational judgement tests

The brilliant learning from Chapter 9 was that you would *under-stand what the questions in situational judgement tests are asking you to do* and that you would *have a clear strategy to minimise your stress and maximise your performance.* Try this test, on your own, in your own time. The answers are in Part 4, Brilliant answers.

Scenario 1
You are a graduate intern on a two-year training programme at the Benign Sunshine Agency. Benign Sunshine is the UK's fifth largest marketing agency and deals with all aspects of clients' marketing, market research, PR and advertising needs.

You are a 'floating' intern and as such you are assigned to projects and to teams when they are likely to have a role for you and when they will have time to brief, coach and train you effectively in their

▶

work area. You also have a dedicated mentor to whom you can go at any time for help and support with regard to your progress, learning and work in the company.

Situation 1

You have joined a team which is preparing to pitch to an existing client to win a contract to provide the PR for a new range of children's books which aim to teach children about environmental issues in an interesting, engaging and fun way. The client is hoping that primary schools will be interested in purchasing the series of books as one of the major topics in the national curriculum at Key Stage 2 is environmental and energy awareness.

The pitch team manager has asked you to take an active role in the pitch presentation to the client representatives. He particularly wants you to talk about your response to, and enjoyment of, the books as you are the youngest member of the team. The pitch is in two days' time.

Review the following responses A to D and indicate which one you believe to be the response to the situation you would be 'most likely to make' and the response to the situation which you would be 'least likely to make'.

Responses:

(A) Prepare a presentation based on a detailed analysis of previous children's books on this topic that have done well and how they were promoted.
(B) Prepare a presentation based on your experiences of learning about the environment as a child and your favourite books on the topic.
(C) Prepare a presentation about how you felt and what questions came into your mind when you read the clients' books.
(D) Read the books to your nieces and nephews and prepare a presentation based on their response to the books.

Situation 2

You have three days to go until the end of a project that you have been working on for the last four weeks in the market research team. By now you would usually have an email or call from your mentor letting you know about your next assignment location or your host team would have asked you to stay on for more time if they required you. However, neither of these things have happened and therefore you are unsure where you are going to be working next week or what your responsibilities will be.

Review the following responses A to D and indicate which one you believe to be the response to the situation you would be 'most likely to make' and the response to the situation which you would be 'least likely to make.'

Responses:

(A) Delay the end of this project for as long as you can.

(B) Ask your current team leader if she can assign some additional tasks to you to continue this placement a little longer.

(C) Do nothing, as you will be able to use the 'downtime' after this project ends to pursue some personal development without having to work on a project for a while.

(D) Email your mentor to remind him that you think you are due to move on to a new posting or project in three days' time.

Situation 3

You have been asked to stay with the market research team for another project. Because of the competence you demonstrated on your last project in the team you have been given overall responsibility for a small piece of market research which Benign Sunshine have been commissioned to do by West Grimsdale Fire & Rescue Service (WGFRS).

The Service wish to find out how many households in their region currently have smoke alarms fitted and are operational and, of those

▶

who don't, how many are willing to fit smoke alarms in the next six months, either with or without incentives.

Review the following responses A to D and indicate which one you believe to be the first response to the situation you would be 'most likely to make' and the response to the situation which you would be 'least likely to make'.

Responses:

(A) Write a script for a telephone interview which your researchers will conduct with a sample of West Grimsdale households.

(B) Find out how many households there are in West Grimsdale and into what social categories they fall.

(C) Book some telephone researchers for three days next week to call households in West Grimsdale.

(D) Ask your team leader if you can have a meeting with the key contact at WGFRS in order to gain clarification on the detailed objectives of the research.

Situation 4

Over the last few weeks you have had sole responsibility for a market research project being conducted by Benign Sunshine on behalf of West Grimsdale Fire & Rescue Service (WGFRS). You have been doing your best to run the project according to the client's requirements but the key contact at WGFRS, Hector Jones, Director of Community Safety, has been a difficult person to work with.

This morning you received an email from Mr Jones stating that he is unhappy with the number and the quality of interviews you have conducted in households in the region and that he will go 'over your head' unless things improve immediately with regard to the running of the project. You believe that Mr Jones has been a little disappointed, and felt undervalued, because Benign Sunshine have put a graduate trainee in charge of his project. This appears to have negatively affected his view all the way through the process.

▷

Review the following responses A to D and indicate which one you believe to be the response to the situation you would be 'most likely to make' and the response to the situation which you would be 'least likely to make'.

Responses:

(A) Call Mr Jones immediately and apologise that he is unhappy. Ask exactly how you can improve the delivery of the project.

(B) Email back and say that you have delivered all aspects of the project as agreed and attach a copy of the original project plan as proof.

(C) Call Mr Jones' diary secretary and ask for a face-to-face meeting to be booked in to clear up the issues raised.

(D) Inform your team leader that Mr Jones is being difficult and over critical so she won't be surprised if she hears from him later.

Scenario 2

You are working as an intern for a production company that specialises in TV history and art documentaries. Your role is to support the staff at the company and learn aspects of the work they do in order to enhance your production skills and eventually apply for a job as a production assistant.

The company is called Knowledgematic. It is a small organisation with two company Directors, four full-time production assistants and one administrator. Specialist Producers and TV Directors are hired on a freelance basis to work on specific projects.

Situation 1

You have been at Knowledgematic for three months and have yet to gain any experience in location filming. All your work has been studio-based and you are very keen to help out on a location shoot as this will enhance your CV for when you begin applying for permanent jobs.

▶

You are aware the company is going to start filming a documentary about the Battle of Hastings next week and the first few weeks of the filming are going to be on location in East Sussex. You are very keen to be assigned to this project. However, Greta Fornelli, one of the company directors has just approached you to ask that you take on a project to sort through and archive the video tapes, DVDs and film footage which is stored in the backroom at the Knowledgematic offices. She says that she thinks it could take a couple of weeks to go through everything, decide on what should be kept and then archive it properly. She would like you to start next week.

Review the following responses A to D and indicate whether you believe the response to be 1 – The most effective response, 2 – The second most effective response, 3 – The third most effective response or 4 – The least effective response. You may assign each rating only once.

Responses:

(A) Be honest with Greta about your wishes and why you feel that it is important to you that you gain some experience on location. Ask her for her view on this and ask her whether there is any chance that you can spend some time on the East Sussex shoot before returning to the office to start your archiving project.

(B) Say you'd rather go to the location shoot in East Sussex as it would support your development more than doing the archiving.

(C) Agree to do the archiving project and ask Greta for a chance today to talk about your learning and development, specifically when you might get to do some location filming.

(D) Agree to do the archiving project – hopefully another chance to experience location filming will arise soon.

▶

Situation 2

It is a Monday morning; you have a busy week planned, with a media networking event tonight and a champagne preview screening of the Battle of Hastings documentary on Wednesday night. Greta Fornelli, one of the directors, has just approached you to say that she would like you to get involved in a location shoot for a Knowledgematic documentary on 'London's Dickensian Past'. The documentary is due to start filming in three days' time and requires three London streets in which to film. Three streets had been located and permission granted for filming. However, they have just found out that there are to be some major gas mains works being undertaken on one of the chosen streets during the time that the filming is due to take place.

Greta has tasked you with finding an alternative street in which to film in time for the first day of filming on Thursday. The requirements for the location are that the street consist of all Victorian or older houses, the street be in East or South East London, that the street furniture (i.e. lamps, etc) are either of the relevant period or unobtrusive, that residents and the local Borough council will give permission for filming and that the street is not one that has a busy through-flow of traffic; a cul-de-sac would be ideal. Greta says that the last time the location scout was given this brief it took her a week to locate the three streets needed.

Review the following responses A to D and indicate whether you believe the response to be 1 – The most effective response, 2 – The second most effective response, 3 – The third most effective response or 4 – The least effective response. You may assign each rating only once.

Responses:

(A) Cancel your attendance at the champagne preview event as you can always view the Battle of Hastings documentary another day in the office when you have more time.

(B) Cancel your attendance at the media networking event tonight.

▶

(C) Call the relevant people and apologise that you won't be able to attend the evening events and say they should give your place to anyone who may be waiting for a ticket.

(D) Tell Greta that you have two evening events planned before Thursday and that given the likely time it will take to find a relevant location perhaps she should assign another person to work alongside you on the task as well.

Situation 3

Knowledgematic have been given an open brief by Channel 5 to deliver a new art documentary strand to appeal to young people aged between 14 and 25 and which will be aired on weeknights at 7.30pm. Steve Grade, one of the Knowledgematic directors, has given you the task of recommending the topic that should be the opening programme in the series. You must choose the one that will have maximum appeal and draw the target viewers in.

You have to choose between three programmes that are currently in production but will all be completed in time for the series opener in a few weeks' time. The programmes are:

- *All You Ever Wanted To Know About Graphic Novels But Were Afraid To Ask* (A detailed look at the life and work of three of the most successful graphic novelists working today, including the creator of a series of novels that have been turned into a Holly-wood blockbuster trilogy.)

- *Graffiti and Street Art: A Modern Rebellion* (Going undercover with Britain's secretive and passionate graffiti artists and revealing the true identity of Bintsy, the most famous and highly-valued street artist in the world.)

- *The Festival Season* (Following an outdoor performance artist, Taylor Hip, working the UK and Europe's summer festivals; joining her as she hangs out with bands, comedians and other performers to share views on art, drugs, wellies and all manner of 'festivally' things.)

▶

Review the following responses A to D and indicate whether you believe the response to be 1 – The most effective response, 2 – The second most effective response, 3 – The third most effective response or 4 – The least effective response. You may assign each rating only once.

Responses:

(A) Research the popularity of the three topics on the internet: looking at 'trending' topics on Twitter, fan sites and other information.

(B) Give your recommendation based on which one most appeals to you as you are not that knowledgeable about art and therefore feel that you are an average viewer in that sense.

(C) Do an online survey of people aged 14 to 25 and ask them which of the titles most appeals to them; recommend the title that is given the most votes.

(D) Look at the viewing figures for previous documentaries on terrestrial TV which had similar topics.

Situation 4

You are helping out on a studio shoot for the documentary entitled 'London's Dickensian Past'. The presenter of the documentary, Professor Edwin Leighton-Hartly has come in to be filmed speaking about and looking at artefacts from Victorian London, presenting them to camera and explaining their uses and manufacture.

Filming is due to commence in 15 minutes or so and you are just helping the professor go through his lines and where he needs to move to as he holds certain objects and as he explains certain things. The idea is that video clips of actors demonstrating the objects in use will be superimposed behind the professor eventually and therefore he needs to be correctly positioned so that his image allows space for the footage to fit behind or beside him. Professor Leighton-Hartly has never done anything like this before and you notice that he is very nervous, his hands are shaking and his voice is trembling whilst you rehearse with him. He suddenly turns to you and says 'I just don't think I can do this; you're going to need to get someone else'.

▶

Review the following responses A to D and indicate whether you believe the response to be 1 – The most effective response, 2 – The second most effective response, 3 – The third most effective response or 4 – The least effective response. You may assign each rating only once.

Responses:

(A) Tell the professor that everyone gets nervous before filming and that you worked with a famous actor the other day who was suffering from performance anxiety just filming a 30-second trailer.

(B) Get the professor a cup of tea and let him sit down for a minute or two to collect himself.

(C) Suggest that the professor takes deep breaths, relaxes his shoulders and imagines that he is in his lecture room back at university, not in a studio at all.

(D) Tell the professor that you're sure he'll be fine and not to worry.

Scenario 3

You are an assistant in a branch of an independent coffee shop called Tradewinds. You have worked in the shop for three months. Tradewinds try to use customer experience to distinguish themselves from larger coffee chains.

Your main responsibilities are as follows:

- Serving food and beverages at the counter, in a helpful and pleasant manner, including making freshly-brewed espresso, latte and cappuccino coffees on demand.

- Ensuring all stock is within its 'use by' or 'best before' date, and rotated on a first-in, first-out basis.

- Checking deliveries for discrepancies, quality and temperature in accordance with the food safety guidelines.

- Operating the cash register, taking money and dealing with credit card transactions.

- Completing all paperwork relating to food safety and stock taking requirements.

▶

Cleaning and preparing the work surfaces, tables and chairs as required throughout the day.

You work either an early (8am to 4pm) or late (12pm to 8pm) shift, 6 days a week. One assistant usually works the late shift and two work the early shift. The branch manager is usually in the shop from 10am to 6pm.

Situation 1

It is 12.30pm on a Friday. A customer has come into the shop and has been browsing the food counter for a few minutes looking rather impatient and dissatisfied. When you asked the customer how you might be able to help them they said that they are unable to eat wheat or dairy and are finding your selection of food limiting as it is mostly sandwiches and the one salad on offer is a cheese salad. They have also asked to purchase a soya latte coffee. Your shop does not offer soya milk as an alternative to cow's milk as there has not been a great demand for it in the past.

Review the following responses A to D and indicate which you believe to be the 'most effective' response to the situation and which the 'least effective'.

Responses:

(A) Apologise to the customer and say that unfortunately there is not much on Tradewinds' menu which will be appropriate for their diet but they could try the healthfood cafe on the High Street.

(B) Say that your colleague would be happy to freshly prepare a salad without any cheese and ask if the customer would be happy to wait for a few moments whilst you find out about the soy latte. Ask *your* manager if you can pop out to the nearby convenience store for some soya milk to make the latte.

(C) Apologise for the lack of soya milk but offer to freshly prepare a salad without any dairy in it for the customer. Point out any other items in the shop that would be appropriate for their diet.

(D) Suggest the customer go to the healthfood cafe on the High Street and, when the customer has gone, suggest to your manager that your branch introduce soya milk as an alternative for customers and make some non-dairy salads for vegans and people with restricted diets.

Situation 2

A new assistant called Danielle started work at the shop last week. You have worked three early shifts with her this week and two lunchtimes, and during these hours she has appeared reluctant to help out with all the duties that are required of her. She is competent and keen with the paperwork and checking off the food deliveries. However she is not taking her fair share of the work when it comes to serving customers and seems to rely on you or other colleagues to take orders and take customers' money whenever possible. You are due to work an early shift with her again today.

Review the following responses A to D and indicate which you believe to be the 'most effective' response to the situation and which the 'least effective'.

Responses:

(A) Say nothing, but try to hang back every now and then when customers come into the shop, giving Danielle the opportunity to serve a customer on her own.

(B) Take the opportunity to talk to Danielle when there is a lull in service this morning. Ask if she is feeling OK about all aspects of the job and whether she would like you to review any processes or tasks with her to remind her what to do. Say that serving customers is probably the most important aspect of the job and it can also be the most rewarding as you get to meet and talk to all sorts of different people.

▶

(C) Say to Danielle that you feel that the responsibility for serving customers is hers as well as yours. State that you don't think it's fair that you continue dealing with the vast majority of customers whilst she only does the paperwork and deliveries behind the scenes.

(D) When there is a chance this morning ask Danielle if she would like to observe you serving a customer. Show her how enjoyable it can be to serve customers by chatting and being friendly to customers and letting her see how they respond.

Situation 3

You have asked your manager if you can work the late shift every day this week as you have to go to a class every morning in order to complete your food hygiene certificate. The shop closes at 7.30pm each day and the final half-hour of the shift is allocated to cashing up (counting the money, recording the amount and putting it in the safe overnight) and cleaning the kitchen area and shop in readiness for the following day. You have learnt on your course that the method of cleaning the kitchen surfaces at Tradewinds is not 'best practice' and to do it properly would add another 10 minutes on to the process.

Review the following responses A to D and indicate which you believe to be the 'most effective' response to the situation and which the 'least effective'.

Responses:

(A) Start cashing up at 7.20pm in order to make sure that you have the full half-hour to spend on the cleaning.

(B) Talk to your manager and ask for an extra 10 minutes pay on the late shift so you can work until 8.10pm and finish the cleaning to the required standards.

(C) Work as fast as you can to complete the cleaning to the required standard and quickly do the cashing up.

(D) Commence the cleaning and cashing up as usual at 7.30pm but tackle the jobs in a reasonable order of priority. You could leave the least hygiene-critical parts of the shop until last, for example the chairs, tables and floor in the customer area. As long as you have wiped these down you could leave a note for the morning shift saying that they need to give the area a more thorough clean first thing in the morning.

Situation 4

It is Saturday lunchtime, the busiest time of the week for your Tradewinds branch. You are located on a busy shopping street and on Saturday many families and couples come in to get a quick sandwich and a hot drink when browsing the high street stores. This Saturday is no exception and you and your two colleagues are busy serving a queue of eight customers. Your colleague is serving the first customer and they are nearly finished paying. You have asked the second customer what they would like. However the third customer in the queue is a pregnant woman who is looking rather pale and is leaning heavily on the counter. The customer behind her is an impatient looking young man in business dress.

Review the following responses A to D and indicate which you believe to be the 'most effective' response to the situation and which the 'least effective'.

Responses:

(A) Ask the customer you are serving to excuse you for a minute. Turn to the pregnant woman and ask her if she is alright and whether she needs to sit down. If she says she does need to sit down then say that you or your colleague will come and take her order at her table so that she needn't stand any longer. Ask the young man behind her whether he is just buying cold food and drinks in which case your colleague can serve him quickly after the second customer.

▶

(B) Finish serving your current customer as quickly as possible in order that the pregnant woman and impatient man don't have to wait too long.

(C) Tell the pregnant woman to take a seat at a table and your colleague or yourself will come and take her order soon.

(D) Ask your colleague to keep serving at the till and go along the line of customers asking each one what their requirements are with regard to hot or cold food and drinks. Ask all those who only require cold food or drink to form a separate queue and serve these people quickly. Ask the other people to take a seat and wait for you to come and serve them in a minute.

Scenario 4

You are working as a Graduate Management Trainee for Leamouth-on-Sea City Council (LoSCC).

Leamouth-on-Sea is a medium-sized city located approximately 60 miles from London on the South Coast of England. Its primary industries are tourism, financial services and call centres. It used to have a thriving commercial and ferry port although this has reduced in size recently with some of the space being reallocated to retail outlets, leisure and water-side recreation.

The LoSCC graduate training programme lasts for three years with 20% of your time spent doing coursework and study for an MSc in Public Service Management at Leamouth University. This works out at approximately one day a week at university. The remainder of your time you are assigned on a project-by-project basis to work for various departments and functions in the council. The projects range in duration from 1 to 9 months. When each project is complete you, your project manager and your graduate mentor complete an assessment of your performance, learning and development needs based on your work on the project.

▶

Situation 1

You are currently working on a project to plan the decorative planting schemes around the city for next year. These planting schemes use seasonal bedding plants, mixed borders and bulb schemes to create colour and interest throughout the year on the city's roadside verges, road islands and central reservations of major roads. Your team have just completed the outline plan for next year but have now heard that, due to Central Government budget cuts, LoSCC has decided to reduce the budget for your project by 50%. You are going, as a representative of the decorative planting project group, to attend a meeting with the Assistant Director of Finance (ADF) and two councillor members of the Countryside and Horticulture Committee where they intend to explain their reasoning further and outline your new budget. Your team have asked you to strongly challenge the budget cut.

Review the following responses A to E and indicate whether you believe the response to be 'very effective', 'effective', 'slightly effective', 'ineffective' or 'counterproductive'. You may assign each rating only once.

Responses:

(A) Send an email to the ADF and the two councillors before the meeting giving a reasoned and evidence-based argument for why the budget cut is not appropriate. Prepare this argument in a bullet-point sheet for you to refer to in the meeting. Include points about voter and visitor reactions to the urban landscape.

(B) Send a copy of Encouraging Wildlife in Inner Cities to each of the people with whom you will be meeting. It is a pamphlet that explains how roadside planting can encourage bats, birds and insects to thrive in the urban environment.

(C) Call the Director of Finance and ask him to attend the meeting as you want to talk to the person with 'the final say'.

(D) Prepare a document outlining this information to take to the meeting.

(E) Collate data on response to the planting schemes' from visitors and residents. Prepare an 'easy-to-digest' handout, for the ADF and the councillors, which outlines the key arguments for keeping the budget as it is. Hand copies of these out at the meeting.

Situation 2

You are currently working in the Parking Services department of LoSCC. You have just started work on a project to propose and plan the introduction of a new residents' parking scheme in West Central Leamouth. In order to have the proposal approved and put out for public consultation, it needs to be passed by the Parking Committee of the council. The project manager (PM) has just approached you and told you that this month's meeting of the Parking Committee has been brought forward by a week in order to work around a bank holiday later in the month. This means that the team need to complete the proposal by 4pm today. Your PM believes the proposal will require 15 person hours to write; it is now 10am and there are 2 of you available to work on the paper.

Review the following responses A to E and indicate whether you believe the response to be 'very effective', 'effective', 'slightly effective', 'ineffective' or 'counterproductive'. You may assign each rating only once.

Responses:

(A) Split the paper into manageable chunks and prioritise these sections. Make sure that you and your colleague complete the high priority section first and leave appendices etc. until last. At least that way you can submit appendices and supplementary information later if they aren't complete by 4pm.

(B) Start writing the proposal immediately; work as hard as you can toget the entire paper written by 4pm.

(C) Ask your Project Manager to consider submitting the proposal to next month's Committee meeting.

(D) Prioritise the sections of the report and share the high priority ones between the two of you, leaving the less important appendices until last. Also email the Committee convener to see if there is any flexibility in the deadline.

(E) Ask your PM to check why the submission has to be done by 4pm today (you assume that no-one will be reading it overnight); ask for an extension to 9am tomorrow morning if at all possible.

Situation 3

Leamouth-on-Sea City Council is in the process of tendering for a new secondary waste management contract. Currently 'Wastewarriors' (a mid-size specialist recycling company) provide the domestic kitchen food waste collection and recycling service for LoSCC. Their contract is due to expire in two months' time and a new contract needs to be awarded for the service. The current provider is competing for the contract along with two other companies.

You are on a project team which is responsible for analysing and comparing the competing bids. The competing companies have all put in closely comparable bids with regard to the statutory criteria of cost and service reliability (i.e. how likely they are to collect the food waste on schedule). Therefore your project manager has asked you to devise a matrix of other possible selection criteria for the council to use to discriminate between the bidders.

Review the following responses A to E and indicate whether you believe the response to be 'very effective', 'effective', 'slightly effective', 'ineffective' or 'counterproductive'. You may assign each rating only once.

Responses:

(A) Consult a range of sources (including other Local Authorities, waste management industry experts, expert websites and previous Losee bid processes) and collate a longlist of possible criteria to present to your PM for discussion.

(B) Brainstorm ideas yourself 'from first principles'.

(C) Ask 'Wastewarriors' to suggest a list of additional selection criteria.

(D) Ask for a meeting or phone call with the LoSCC Head of Waste Management and pick their brains as to what criteria might be appropriate.

(E) Gather a few other team members together for a brainstorming session to generate as many possible criteria as you can. Check this list against the expert information on the internet to provide a realistic list for presentation to your PM.

Situation 4

During your study day at Leamouth University this week, you got chatting to one of the other LoSCC graduate trainees. His name is Graham Knight and he started on the training scheme and the MSc at the same time as you. You know him reasonably well although you have never worked on the same project at LoSCC and only usually meet up on your study days.

Graham told you in confidence that he is struggling to cope with the demands of the MSc course work, revising for the end-of-year exams and the tight deadlines on a project at work. He tells you that he is thinking of dropping out of the LoSCC programme but finishing the MSc, although he will have to pay back all of his tuition fees which were covered by LoSCC.

Review the following responses A to E and indicate whether you believe the response to be 'very effective', 'effective', 'slightly effective', 'ineffective' or 'counterproductive'. You may assign each rating only once.

Responses:

(A) Arrange a time next week for a sit down/ lunch with Graham to talk through his problems in detail. Let him get all his problems 'off his chest' and then help him start to generate solutions to his time management challenges and ways that he can increase his personal resilience.

(B) Take him out for a drink and help him forget about his troubles and unwind for at least one night.

(C) Feel relieved that there will be one less person to compete with for Losee management jobs and wish him luck in the future.

(D) Suggest Graham talks his problems through with his graduate mentor.

(E) Suggest a time next week when you will be available for a longer chat with Graham. Bring along some time management/stress management books to show Graham. Listen to his problems in detail.

Reproduced with permission from www.assessmentday.co.uk

Chapter 10 Personality tests

The brilliant learning from Chapter 10 was that you would *understand what personality tests are asking you to do* and that you would *be clear about how to tackle them*. Register on the Assessment Day website so you can take their online personality test. Once completed, you will get some feedback online. **www.assessmentday.co.uk/**

PART 4

Brilliant
answers

Here are the worked answers to the questions which tested your Brilliant learning.

Chapter 1 What are psychometric tests?

The brilliant learning from Chapter 1 was that you would understand five different types of tests which are commonly used by employers. See how you got on:

1.1 **If an employer uses psychometric tests as part of the recruitment process they will use the whole range of tests available.**

False: employers only use the psychometrics which measure what is important in the job on offer; there is no need to measure anything else.

1.2 **Verbal reasoning tests only look at your understanding of the passage you have to read.**

False: verbal reasoning tests your ability to work through a problem systematically, using reason and logic to get to the only correct answer. If it is simply your reading ability they want to test, that's the test they will use.

1.3 **You will come across the same kind of reasoning tests whether the employer is in public or private sector and even across engineering and banking.**

True: reasoning ability doesn't change across employer, so you will come across similar tests irrespective of whether the employer is public or private sector or indeed whether the sector is banking or health.

1.4 **Either you get reasoning or you don't – practising won't help.**

False: practising helps you to be familiar with what the tests demand of you, so you can focus on dealing with the test rather than using up all your energy working out how on earth you're going to tackle it.

1.5 Situational judgement tests measure skills like problem-solving and team-working, which can transfer across employer and sector.

True: many SJTs test these kinds of skills which readily transfer across different jobs and different employers.

1.6 Personality tests can give you a real insight into the kind of person you are so can be useful if you don't get the job in telling you something about whether that job would have suited you.

True: this is particularly true where you get written feedback, but even where you simply do the test, it makes you think about what makes you tick – and whether that would honestly have fitted in with the job on offer.

1.7 Psychometrics are the best way of selecting for a job.

False: psychometrics are a good way to measure the mind, but should be used alongside other selection techniques (application form or interview) to get a full picture.

1.8 You can't really do a situational judgement test unless you've already worked in that role.

False: you don't need prior knowledge to tackle a SJT – but it can help to picture yourself already doing the job if you are stuck for an answer.

1.9 Public and private sector use the same reasoning tests.

True: that's because they both prize the ability to reason.

1.10 Personality tests help you check whether the job is really right for you.

True: because they are so thorough, you'll really have to think about who you are – and that helps you to work out whether you are cut out for the job.

Chapter 2 Why do employers use psychometric tests?

The brilliant learning from Chapter 2 was firstly that you would *understand why employers use psychometric tests for selection and talent management* and secondly that you would *know how psychometric tests are used alongside other selection techniques*. Here are the worked answers:

2.1 **Employers use psychometrics so as to get the best person for the job.**

True: employers use them as objective measures to ensure they make a good appointment.

2.2 **Psychometrics indicate that if you're good in the test you'll be good in the job.**

True: research proves there is a link between performance in a test and on the job.

2.3 **Employers like to reject people and use tests as an excuse to do just that.**

False: employers want to hire the right person for the job and tests help with that. They can also help with filtering out people who would be wholly unsuited for the job advertised.

2.4 **They just make these quizzes up; they can put anything down and call it a test.**

False: there's a lot of psychological science behind psychometric tests.

2.5 **The only time you'll have to do a psychometric test is to get started in your career.**

False: psychometrics are commonly used for promotion boards to high levels in a company.

2.6 **Employers use psychometrics alongside other selection methods such as interview.**

True: at the very least you can expect an interview or application form to be used alongside a test.

2.7 **You've got to get a much higher score than just the benchmark on every test.**

False: you do have to hit the benchmark in every test, but it's your performance overall that counts.

2.8 **Doing a great application is more important than passing an online test.**

False: for some employers, you can't submit an application until you have passed the online test.

2.9 **Employers sometimes sequence tests; you have to pass one to get access to the next.**

True: the selection process can comprise several stages, with applicants filtered out at each one.

2.10 **Thinking about how you got on helps you make sense of career decisions.**

True: your performance in psychometric tests can indicate where your preferences lie.

Chapter 3 What to expect and how to prepare

The brilliant learning from Chapter 3 was firstly that you would *understand how preparing for tests can help you* and secondly that you *would be able to adopt a mindset which minimises nerves and maximises your performance.*

Answers (a) are unrealistic and panicky, answers (c) won't help you progress at all.

For each of these scenarios, the correct answer is (b) because in doing these actions, you prepare for the tests and adopt a mindset which helps you do your best in the tests.

Please note that this is in no way a scientifically rigorous personality test – just a light-hearted way of checking you'd got the message.

3.1 The online tests for the FabGrad mega-scheme close at the end of November.

(b) Factor in a couple of practice sessions and a test date, working around other commitments.

3.2 It's mid-November; your laptop is acting weird and so is everyone in your house.

(b) Look into booking a private study space and reserving a computer for last week of November.

3.3 You log on to the FabGrad website, start the clock and can't answer anything.

(b) Breathe out and focus.

3.4 You somehow get through the FabGrad online test and immediately you:

(b) Take half an hour to work out what was OK and what needs a bit more practice.

Chapter 4 What if I don't get through?

The brilliant learning from Chapter 4 was that you would identify how to use your experience of psychometric tests for personal and professional development. As this is all about your unique learning experience, there is no right answer as such. There are however, two key outputs from the tasks, which are:

Task 1 – Use an online career planning tool.

You should have registered either for the National Careers Service skills health check or the Prospects career planner. You can keep going back online as you progress in your career thinking.

Task 2 – Reflective learning.

The final section of the process should have led you to identify a change action you will implement at some point in the future. Once you've done that, go back to the reflection and go through the cycle again. You can of course work through the reflective learning cycle as frequently and as widely as you wish. This is an entirely personal document but you might find you want to use some of your reflection as example material in an application form or interview.

Chapter 6 Verbal reasoning tests

The brilliant learning from Chapter 6 was that you would understand what the questions in verbal reasoning tests are asking you to do and would have a clear strategy to minimise your stress and maximise your performance. Here are the worked answers:

Q1 **The Bilderberg Group has critics on both sides of the ideological spectrum.**

True: summarises the 8th and 9th sentences. Right-wing critics being one side and left-wing activists being the other.

Q2 **Representatives from the media are not allowed to attend the Bilderberg Group conference.**

False: while the fourth sentence states that 'Reporters, however, are not invited' the second sentence states that conference participants include 'newspaper editors'.

Q3 **The Bilderberg Group was created as a private forum to set Europe and America's political and financial agenda.**

False: while many conspiracy theories promote this idea, the fifth and sixth sentences state that the Group was established to promote understanding and does not set policy.

Q4 **Topics discussed at Bilderberg Group conferences have included the invasion of Iraq.**

Cannot say: as the conferences are private, there is no way of knowing what was discussed.

Q5 **Because its delegates are not elected, the Bilderberg Group's activities are widely believed to be undemocratic.**

Cannot say: both sides of the argument are argued in the last sentence. We are not told either way if this view is 'widely believed'.

Q6 **Trieste, Trentina and Istria were reunified with Italy following the Treaty of Versailles.**

Cannot say: while the third sentence lists these areas as Italian territories, and the fifth sentence states that the Treaty of Versailles 'satisfied most of Italy's irredentist claims' the passage does not expressly state that these territories became part of Italy.

Q7 **Borders imposed in 1919 by the Treaty of Versailles resulted in twentieth century conflicts.**

True: both World War II and the Bosnian War were the result of irredentist claims over borders.

Q8 **Irredentist movements advocate the annexation of territories only on the grounds of prior historical possession.**

False: there are a variety of reasons given in the first sentence.

Q9 **Yugoslavia was created following the Second World War to provide a homeland for Bosnians, Serbs and Croats.**

False: Yugoslavia was created after the First World War. All the examples in the second half of the passage pertain to the Treaty of Versailles.

Q10 **Although originally an Italian movement, irredentist claims are now being made in other countries.**

True: the last two sentences mention irredentist claims in East Africa and the Near East.

Q11 **The global water crisis has resulted in less of the world's population having access to fresh water.**

Cannot say: the second sentence tells us that more people in developing countries have access to clean water than before

(2 billion more than in 1990), however we are not told if more or fewer people in developed countries have access to fresh water. So we are not given the whole picture and therefore we cannot say.

Q12 **The irrigation of crops comprises the majority of groundwater usage.**

Cannot say: the passage states that 70% of the world's freshwater use is for agriculture and that groundwater is used to irrigate crops. It does not follow that 70% of groundwater is used for farming.

Q13 **Despite increasing rainfall in some areas, climate change is the main cause of the global water crisis.**

Cannot say: the passage does not cite a primary cause for the crisis.

Q14 **The main impediment to desalination is expense.**

Cannot say: the passage states that 'The process's high costs however limit its wide-spread adoption'. However it does not follow that this is the main impediment.

Q15 **Both technological innovation and diplomacy are needed to tackle the world's water crisis.**

True: the 11th sentence says 'The solution to the global water crisis lies predominantly in new technologies.' The last sentence goes on to say that 'Organising bodies and treaties are also needed . . .'. So we are told that both technology and diplomacy (organising bodies and treaties) are needed.

Q16 **One of the advantages of Esperanto is that it is universally easy to learn.**

Cannot say: because it is based on European languages it is indeed easier for speakers of European languages to learn Esperanto, however we are not told if others find it 'easy' or not.

Q17 **Dr Zamenhof's goal was to replace ethnic languages with the universal language of Esperanto.**

False: the third sentence refers to Zamenhof's goal of an 'international auxiliary language' – he did not aim to replace ethnic languages.

Q18 **Esperanto's lack of an associated culture or homeland can be viewed as both an asset and a disadvantage.**

True: as stated in the 8th sentence.

Q19 **Contemporary Esperanto speakers do not share a common vision of the language's purpose.**

True: the sixth sentence describes two different visions for Esperanto.

Q20 **Loglan is a more logically constructed language than Esperanto.**

Cannot say: while the last sentence states that Loglan is based on logic, the fifth sentence describes Esperanto's grammar as having 'logical rules' and the two languages are not directly compared. We cannot say which of the two is the most logically constructed.

Q21 **Prescription drug abusers are typically young adults who have access to the drugs at home.**

Cannot say: the passage does not state whether prescription drug abusers come from a specific demographic, though the fifth sentence does refer to young adults.

Q22 **The pharmaceutical industry has made opioid painkillers highly addictive to enhance their profits.**

False: while the last sentence refers to the fact that opioids are lucrative for pharmaceutical companies, the third sentence states that they are only addictive in one percent of patients when used properly. So it is not true to say they are 'highly addictive'.

Q23 **Prescription drug abuse in the United States is generally attributed to the availability of strong opioids.**

True: the second sentence states 'most experts concur that the cause is the increased availability of powerful new opioid analgesics.'

Q24 **The erroneous belief that there are fewer risks associated with taking prescription drugs recreationally is prevalent.**

True: paraphrases the sixth sentence.

Q25 Medical professionals do not support proposed government restrictions on the prescription of opioids.

Cannot say: while the 9th sentence states that 'some healthcare professionals have expressed concern that restricting opioids . . . would have an adverse effect' it is not possible to say what ALL medical professionals think or support.

Q26 Corvids' feeding behaviour indicates that they have some awareness of what their competitors are thinking.

True: summarises the fifth and sixth sentences regarding the re-hiding of food.

Q27 The social function of intellect theory states that corvid intelligence developed as a result of their complex social structure.

True: The 8th sentence defines this theory as being applied to other species, such as corvids.

Q28 Although they lack a common ancestor, primates and corvids acquired their intelligence under the same evolutionary processes.

Cannot say: while this is the definition of convergent evolution, the final sentence indicates that not all scientists believe that primates and corvids evolved convergently, so there is no consensus.

Q29 Corvids' cognitive abilities are the result of both brain structure and social structure.

Cannot say: the 8th sentence cites the social function of intellect theory but this is just 'hypothesised' not stated as fact. Also the 10th sentence refers to the nidopallium within the birds' brains, but again this is said to be 'believed' by scientists to fulfil a cognitive function.

Q30 A corvid's nidopallium is smaller, but more powerful, than a primate's neocortex.

Cannot say: while overall brain size is compared, the size of the nidopallium and neocortex are not compared. Furthermore, the 10th sentence states that scientists 'believe' the nidopallium fulfils a similar function to the neocortex. This is not an established fact.

Chapter 7 Numerical/non-verbal reasoning

The brilliant learning from Chapter 7 was that you would *understand what the questions in non-verbal/numerical reasoning tests are asking you to do* and would *have a clear plan of attack to minimise your stress and maximise your performance*. Here are the worked answers:

Q1 **What was the 2010 percentage change in the value of the Pacific Rim holding between October and November (to the nearest percent)?**

Step 1 Calculate the October value.
The information that you need is shown in the pie chart.
£37.5 million × 20% = £7.5 million

Step 2 Calculate the November value
The information that you need is shown in the graph.
50.0 × £100,000 = £5 million

Step 3 Calculate the % difference
7.5 − 5.0 = 2.5
100 × (2.5 / 7.5) = 33.33 less.
Or another way: simply divide 5.0 by 7.5 to get 0.6667, which can be interpreted as a 33.3% reduction.

Thus the correct answer is (e) 33% less.

Q2 **What was the ratio of Pacific Rim: Southern Pacific holdings in October 2010?**

The information that you need is shown in the pie chart.

Step 1 Put these October %'s into a ratio
20%:35% = 20:35

Step 2   Simplify the ratio, looking at the available answers.
20:35 = 4:7

Thus the correct answer is (e) 4:7.

Q3 In October 2010 which two Pacific Bond fund holdings when combined had the same value as Southern Pacific holdings?

The information that you need is shown in the graph.

Step 1   Work out the percentages of the options listed and see which is equal to 35%
Northern Pacific + Central Pacific = 33%
Central Pacific + Pacific Rim = 35%
Pacific Mixed + Pacific Rim = 32%
Pacific Mixed + Northern Pacific = 30%
Pacific Rim + Northern Pacific = 38%

Thus the correct answer is (b) Central Pacific and Pacific Rim.

Q4 Which of the following represents the largest amount?

Step 1   In this one it is not obvious which ones are going to be wrong and therefore able to be discounted, so we must calculate the value of each option:
(a)   October's Pacific Mixed holding = 4.5 million
(b)   Average November value of each of the 5 holdings = 7.2 million
(c)   November value of holdings in Northern Pacific = 6.14 million
(d)   70% of November's value of holdings in Southern Pacific = 6.47 million
(e)   Average December value of each of the 5 holdings = 7 million

Thus the correct answer is (b) Average November value of each of the 5 holdings.

Q5 **In October 2010 what fraction of the total Pacific Bond did the Northern Pacific and Pacific Mixed fund holdings represent?**

The information that you need is shown in the pie chart.

Step 1   Add the Northern Pacific and Pacific Mixed %'s
$18\% + 12\% = 30\%$

Step 2   Express this figure as a fraction
$30 / 100 = 3 / 10$

Thus the correct answer is (d) 3 / 10

Q6 **For Weeks 1 and 3, across all 5 stores combined, what was the difference (in units) between Actual and Target sales volumes?**

Step 1   Calculate the total Week 1 and Week 3 sales across the 5 stores

Week 1: $20 + 30 + 25 + 15 + 5 = 95$
Week 3: $35 + 40 + 24 + 12 + 9 = 120$

Step 2   Calculate the total Week 1 and Week 3 targets across the 5 stores

Week 1: $15 + 20 + 20 + 10 + 10 = 75$
Week 3: $35 + 35 + 30 + 15 + 15 = 130$

Step 3   Calculate the difference for Weeks 1 and 3

Week 1: $95 - 75 = 20$ over target
Week 3: $120 - 130 = 10$ under target

Thus the correct answer is (e) 20 over target (Week 1); 10 under target (Week 3)

Q7 **Over the three week period, which store achieved the highest sales per sales staff member?**

Step 1   Calculate each store's total sales
Use the Actual sales figures for each of the 3 weeks, as follows:

Redcliff	$20 + 20 + 35 = 75$
Ather	$30 + 40 + 40 = 110$
Wilkington	$25 + 18 + 24 = 67$
Trew	$15 + 14 + 12 = 41$
Tunston	$5 + 6 + 9 = 20$

Step 2 Calculate each store's average sales per sales staff member, as follows:

Redcliff	$75 / 8 = 9.4$
Ather	$110 / 9 = 12.2$
Wilkington	$67 / 5 = 13.4$
Trew	$41 / 8 = 5.1$
Tunston	$20 / 6 = 3.3$

Thus the correct answer is (c) Wilkington.

Q8 **Next year staff numbers are to be reduced by 1 at stores with 6 or fewer staff, and by 2 staff at all other stores. What will be the average monthly target per staff member across all 5 stores if the regional target (across the 5 stores) is £168,000?**

Step 1 Calculate the new staff numbers

Redcliff	$8-2 = 6$ staff
Ather	$9-2 = 7$ staff
Wilkington	$5-1 = 4$ staff
Trew	$8-2 = 6$ staff
Tunston	$6-1 = 5$ staff

Step 2 Calculate the average target per staff member

Average target / total number of staff $= 168,000 / 28 = £6,000$

Thus the correct answer is (b) £6,000

Q9 **The Western region's overall sales (£120,000) were in a ratio of 3:2 to the Eastern region's sales which itself had half the sales of the Northern and Southern regions combined. What were the total sales of all 4 regions?**

Step 1   Calculate each region's sales
Eastern region's sales = 2 × 120,000 / 3 = 80,000
Northern + Southern regions' sales = 80,000 × 2
= 160,000

Step 2   Calculate the total sales
120,000 + 80,000 + 160,000 = 360,000

Thus the correct answer is (e) £360,000.

Q10 **All sales in the three week period were based on an average £9.50 reduction in the sales price of the units sold. What was the total saving made by customers who bought units over the 3 week period (to the nearest £100)?**

Step 1   Calculate the total sales
We could use the working from Q6 to obtain Week 1 and Week 3 sales totals.
Week 2 sales = 20 + 40 + 18 + 14 + 6 = 98
Total sales = Week 1 + Week 2 + Week 3
= 95 + 98 + 120 = 313

Step 2   Calculate the amount saved 313 × £9.50 = £2,973.50

Step 3   (to the nearest £100)
£2,973.50 = £3,000

Thus the correct answer is (a) £3,000.

brilliant tip

When summing numbers from a column or row, be careful not to take numbers from an adjacent category. It is also a good idea to enter the numbers as you go straight into your calculator, instead of writing out the sum on your rough paper then performing the calculation. This will reduce the number of stages in your working and save time and reduce the potential for input errors.

Q11 **Which sector experienced the highest sales for Quarters 1, 2 and 3 combined?**

The information that you need is shown in the graph 'Consultancy income by sector'.

Step 1   Calculate each sector's sales for Quarters 1, 2 and 3 combined

Telecommunications = 30 + 27 + 25 = 82

Utilities = 35 + 20 + 20 = 75

Manufacturing = 21 + 32 + 30 = 83

Financial = 25 + 29 + 30 = 84

Retail = 23 + 30 + 25 = 78

Thus the correct answer is (d) Financial.

Q12 **Quarter 4's income per sector is in the same ratio as Quarter 3, and the consultancy income from the Financial sector is £33,000. What is the consultancy income from the Utilities sector?**

The information that you need is shown in the graph 'Consultancy income by sector'.

Step 1   Find the Quarter 3 ratios

Utilities: Financial = 20.30 = 2.3

Step 2   Apply this ratio to the Utilities sector

Utilities income = £33,000 × 2 / 3 = £22,000

Thus the correct answer is (c) £22,000.

Q13 **For Quarters 1 and 3 combined, which two Manufacturing sector consultants had incomes in the ratio 2:3?**

The information that you need is shown in the table.

Step 1   Calculate each Consultant's combined Quarter 1 and Quarter 3 income, as shown below:

Consultant	Quarter 1	Quarter 3	Combined
David	4,000	5,000	9,000
Peter	6,000	7,000	13,000

Consultant	Quarter 1	Quarter 3	Combined
Sarah	6,000	5,500	11,500
Jane	4,000	7,500	11,500
Harry	1,000	5,000	6,000

The only possible 2:3 ratio is between Harry and David (6,000:9,000) Thus the correct answer is (a) Harry and David.

Q14 **The Manufacturing sector income from the five consultants is supplemented by the work of an associate consultant. What was the associate consultant's income from the Manufacturing sector across Quarters 1 to 3?**

The information that you require here is shown in the table.

Step 1 Calculate the total manufacturing income from the 5 consultants
Q1 Total = 21,000
Q2 Total = 28,000
Q3 Total = 30,000

Total income (Quarters 1 to 3) = 79,000

The information that you require next is shown in the graph.

Step 2 Calculate the overall consultancy income from the manufacturing sector
21 + 32 + 30 = 83,000

Step 3 Calculate the supplementary income
83,000 − 79,000 = 4,000

Thus the correct answer is (b) £4,000.

Q15 **The total quarterly income target, starting with £115,000 for Quarter 1, increased by 20% for each subsequent quarter. In Quarter 3 what was the difference between actual income and the target?**

Step 1   Calculate the target for Quarter 3, based upon the
Quarter 2 target
Quarter 2 target = £115,000 × 120% = £138,000
Quarter 3 target = £138,000 × 120% = £165,600

The information that you require next is shown in the graph.

Step 2   Calculate the Quarter 3 income
Quarter 3 income (000's) = 25 + 20 + 30 + 30 + 25
= 130

Step 3   Calculate the difference in Quarter 3 between income
and target
130,000 − 165,600 = 35,600 under-performance

Thus the correct answer is (e) £35,600 under-performance.

Q16 **Simon and Jessica have travel allowances of 60p and
44p per mile respectively. Simon and Jessica each travel on
average 25 miles and 30 miles respectively per sales visit.
How much travel allowance is claimed in total by these two
sales managers in August?**

Step 1   Calculate Simon and Jessica's total mileage in August
Simon = 60p × 70 × 25 = £1,050
Jessica = 44p × 85 × 30 = £1,122

Step 2   Calculate Simon and Jessica's combined travel allowance
payment
£1,050 + £1,122 = £2,172

Thus the correct answer is (d) £2,172.

Q17 **If the percentage change in sales visits between
September and October (projected) continues for
November, what will Jessica and Kim's number of complete
sales visits be in November?**

Step 1   Calculate the % change for Jessica and Kim
Jessica = 81 / 90 − 10% decrease
Kim = 70 / 62 = 12.903% increase

Step 2 Calculate each sales manager's number of visits for
November
Jessica = 81 × 90% = 72.9 visits
Kim = 70 × 112.903% = 79.03 visits

Step 3 This step can catch out people. The question asks for
'complete sales visits' and 0.9 is not a complete visit. So
Jessica completed 72 visits. Don't be tempted to round up.

Thus the correct answer is (d) 72 visits (Jessica); visits 79 (Kim).

Q18 **If the margin of error on October's projected client
visits is +/− 15%, what are the ranges for each sales
manager (rounded to the nearest whole visit)?**

Step 1 Calculate the 85% and 115% figures for each sales
manager
Simon (to the nearest whole visit)
95 × 85% = 80.75 = 81
95 × 115% = 109.25 =109
Note that already we have eliminated 3 of the possible
5 answers.

Step 2 Jessica:
81 × 85% = 68.85 = 69
81 × 115% = 93.15 = 93
Kim
70 × 85% = 59.5 = 60
70 × 115% = 80.5 = 81

Thus the correct answer is (d) 81–109 (Simon); 69–93 (Jessica);
60–81 (Kim).

⁕ **brilliant** tip

Note the difference between 'round to the nearest whole visit' and
'give the number of complete visits'. This is the difference between
rounding to the nearest integer (could be up or down) and ignoring
any part-complete events (will always be rounding down).

Q19 **Jessica, who travelled 3,500 miles in July, travelled an extra 10 miles per client visit compared to Simon. What was the total number of miles Simon travelled in July?**

Step 1   Let x = Jessica's average mileage per client visit
July visits = 70 = 3,500/ x
x = 3,500 / 70 = 50 miles per visit

Step 2   Calculate Simon's average mileage per client visit
50 − 10 = 40 miles per visit

Step 3   Calculate the total number of miles Simon travelled in July
40 × 65 = 2,600 miles

Thus the correct answer is (b) 2,600 miles.

Q20 **The average order values per client visit are £145, £135 and £125 for Simon, Jessica and Kim respectively. Which sales managers generated the highest and lowest order values in June?**

Step 1   Calculate each sales manager's client sales for June, as follows:

Simon	50 visits in June	50 × £145 = £7,250
Jessica	45 visits in June	45 × £135 = £6,075
Kim	60 visits in June	60 × £125 = £7,500

Thus the correct answer is (a) Kim (most); Jessica (least).

Q21 **Which subsidiary will pay the lowest amount in dividends (interim and final dividends combined)?**

Step 1   Calculate the total dividends payable per share for each subsidiary
Subsidiary 1 = 6.2 + 15.8 = 22
Subsidiary 2 = 8.5 + 10.5 = 19
Subsidiary 3 = 9 + 46 = 55
Subsidiary 4 = 15 + 10 = 25
Subsidiary 5 = 11 + 25 = 36

Step 2   Calculate the total payable for each subsidiary
Subsidiary 1 = 22 cents × 3 million shares = \$660,000
Subsidiary 2 = 19 cents × 3.5 million shares = \$665,000
Subsidiary 3 = 55 cents × 12 million shares = \$6,600,000
Subsidiary 4 = 25 cents × 2.6 million shares = \$650,000
Subsidiary 5 = 36 cents × 20 million shares = \$7,200,000

Thus the correct answer is (d) Subsidiary 4.

Q22 Which 2 or 3 subsidiaries had combined sales of 1,890.8 million?

Step 1   This question is best answered by a process of elimination:

Review the last number in each sales figure. The sales figures for Subsidiary 1 and Subsidiary 2 end in '4' and the others end in zero.

Since the total ends in '8' both Subsidiary 1 and Subsidiary 2 must be included in the answer (as 4 + 4 = 8).

At this stage you can see that only one of the possible answers includes Subsidiary 1 and Subsidiary 2. If you wanted to complete the sum to double-check, do so. Subsidiary 1 + 2 + 5 = 1,124 + 3,334 + 14,450 = 18,908 (100,000s).

Thus the correct answer is (c) Subsidiaries 1, 2 and 5.

Q23 Over the next year, Subsidiary 5's sales are expected to drop by a fifth whilst its number of staff is expected to increase by 15%. What will be the percentage change in the sales per member of staff from Year 1 to the next?

Step 1   Calculate next year's changes in the Subsidiary 5 data
Sales 14,450 × 4 / 5 = 11,560
Number of staff = 13,292 × 115% = 15,285.8

Step 2   Calculate next year's sales per member of staff
11,560 / 15,285.66 = 0.756 (in \$100,000s).

Step 3 Calculate this year's sales per member of staff
14,450 / 13,292 = 1.087 (in $100,000s).

Step 4 Calculate the % change in the sales per member of staff
0.756 / 1.087 = 0.6955, which is a 30.4% drop.

✦ brilliant tip

Note we must divide 0.756 by 1.087, not the other way round,
because the question asks us to go from Year 1 to next year. The
calculation depends on what we take as the reference point. In full,
the calculation is (1.087 − 0.756) / 1.087 = 30.4%.

Thus the correct answer is (d) 30%.

Q24 **What is the ratio of Subsidiary 4's interim dividend per
share compared to Subsidiary 5's final dividend per share?**

This is a fairly straightforward one.

Step 1 Put the figures from the table into a ratio 15:25

Step 2 Simplify the ratio 3:5

Thus the correct answer is (d) 3:5.

Q25 **What is the lowest payroll per member of staff (across
the 5 subsidiaries)?**

Step 1 Calculate the average payroll for each subsidiary
Subsidiary 1 = 12,700,000 / 555 = 22,883
Subsidiary 2 = 40,900,000 / 1,722 = 23,751
Subsidiary 3 = 28,900,000 / 1,343 = 21,519
Subsidiary 4 = 57,000,000 / 2,824 = 20,184
Subsidiary 5 = 435,500,000 / 13,292 = 32,764

Thus the correct answer is (e) £20,184.

Q26 **If profit before tax increases by 15% for Competitor
B and decreases by 8% for Competitor A, what is the
difference between Competitor A and Competitor B's
corporation tax payments (to the nearest £ million)?**

brilliant tip

Don't be caught out by the fact that the question lists Competitor B first, when you might be expecting to see Competitor A then Competitor B. This is intended to throw those not paying attention.

Step 1 Add 15% to Competitor B's profit before tax
$112 \times 115\% = 128.8$

Step 2 Decrease Competitor A's profit before tax by 8%
$90 \times 92\% = 82.8$

Step 3 Calculate the difference in corporation tax (at 30%)
$(128.8 - 82.8) \times 30\% = 13.8 = £14$ million (to the nearest £million)

Thus the correct answer is (c) £14 million.

Q27 **Competitor B and Competitor C choose to declare their Revenues in US dollars ($) and Euros (€) respectively. What are these figures? (Use the exchange rates £1 = $1.66; £1 = €1.15).**

Step 1 Calculate Competitor b revenue in $
$632 \times 1.66 = \$1,049$

Step 2 Calculate Competitor C revenues in Euros
$600 \times 1.15 \times = €690.$

Thus the correct answer is (b) $1,049 million (Competitor B); €690 million (Competitor C).

Q28 **What would be the difference in Euros if Competitor A used an exchange rate of £1 = €1.20, rather than £1 = €1.15, when calculating its profit after tax?**

Step 1 Calculate the difference in the exchange rate
$1.20 - 1.15 = €0.05$

Step 2 Calculate the difference in Euros
$€0.05 \times 63 = €3.15$ million

Thus the correct answer is (e) €3.15 million.

Q29 **What was the average gross profit across the 3 competitors (to the nearest £10 million)?**

Step 1 Calculate the total gross profit 128 + 148 + 147 = 423

Step 2 Calculate the average 423 / 3 = 141

Step 3 To the nearest £10 million = £140 million

Thus the correct answer is (a) £140 million.

Q30 **Competitor C moves to a country charging 15% corporation tax and corporation tax falls to 22% for Competitors A and B. What is the total corporation tax payable for the 3 competitors (based upon the profit before tax figures shown)?**

Step 1 Calculate the corporation tax payable for each competitor
Competitor A = 90 × 22% = 19.8
Competitor B = 112 × 22% = 24.6
Competitor C = 117 × 15% = 17.6

Step 2 Calculate the total corporation tax payable 19.8 + 24.6 + 17.6 = £62 million

Thus the correct answer is (a) £62 million.

Chapter 8 Inductive, abstract and diagrammatic reasoning

The brilliant learning from Chapter 8 was that you would *understand what the questions in inductive, abstract and diagrammatic reasoning tests are asking you to do* and you would *have a clear plan of attack to minimise your stress and maximise your performance.* Here are the worked answers:

Q1 **What comes next in the sequence?**

Answer = D

Rule 1: The triangle moves clockwise 1 place, then 2 places, then 3 places and so on, around the circle.

Rule 2: The triangle alternates between shaded and unshaded.

Rule 3: The number of shaded segments in the circle increases by one each time.

Q2 **What comes next in the sequence?**

Answer = B

Rule 1: The shape at the top alternates between the top left and top right-hand corners.

Rule 2: The number of edges of the shape indicates how many bricks should be added to the next box.

Rule 3: The number of shaded bricks per box increases by two each time.

Q3 **What comes next in the sequence?**

Answer = A

Rule 1: The total number of edges in each box is equal to ten.

Rule 2: The last shape in each box is the first shape of the next box.

Rule 3: The shading moves one place to the right each time and then begins again from the left.

Q4 **What comes next in the sequence?**

Answer = D

Rule 1: The minutes (long) hand rotates 5 hours counterclockwise each time.

Rule 2: The hour (short) hand rotates 3 places clockwise each time.

Rule 3: The circle at the centre of the clock alternates between black and white.

Q5 **What comes next in the sequence?**

Answer = A

Rule 1: The notches move 1 place clockwise around the edge of the box and each time increase by one.

Rule 2: The centre symbol is mirrored horizontally each time.

Rule 3: The number of lines in the centre symbol increases by one every two boxes.

Q6 **What comes next in the sequence?**

Answer = C

Rule 1: When the circuit is complete (the bottom connection is closed) the bulb lights up. When the circuit is broken (bottom connection is open) the bulb does not light up.

Rule 2: The arrows on the left of the circuit alternate between pointing up and down.

Rule 3: The box at the top of the circuit increases in size each time.

Q7 **What comes next in the sequence?**

Answer = D

Rule 1: The rings alternate between cross-hatched and black.

Rule 2: The missing quarter moves one place counterclockwise each time.

Rule 3: Every second box has a star in the missing quarter.

Q8 **What comes next in the sequence?**

Answer = E

Rule 1: The number of diagonal lines at the bottom of the box increases by three each time.

Rule 2: The total number of edges on the shapes is equal to one less than the total number of lines.

Rule 3: The shapes alternate between shaded and unshaded.

Q9 What comes next in the sequence?

Answer = E

Rule 1: The small black circle rotates counterclockwise around the large circle each time.

Rule 2: The arrow rotates 135° counterclockwise each time.

Rule 3: The large circle alternates between having a white trim and no trim.

Q10 What comes next in the sequence?

Answer = E

Rule 1: The key base alternates between circular and hexagonal.

Rule 2: The hole in the key is circular, square then hexagonal. The pattern then begins again.

Rule 3: The key flips horizontally each time.

Q11 What comes next in the sequence?

Answer = D

Rule 1: One box rotates 45° counterclockwise each time.

Rule 2: The other box rotates 90° each time.

Rule 3: When both boxes overlap, the overlapping area is shaded.

Q12 What comes next in the sequence?

Answer = B

Rule 1: Each shape moves two places to the right each time. When they reach the right end of the line, they begin again from the left-hand side.

Rule 2: The final shape in each sequence is always shaded.

Rule 3: The other shading moves one place to the left each time.

Q13 What comes next in the sequence?

Answer = B

Rule 1: The black circle moves 4 places clockwise each time.

Rule 2: The missing line moves one corner clockwise each time.

Rule 3: The thick line moves two places counterclockwise each time.

Q14 What comes next in the sequence?

Answer = E

Rule 1: The symbol moves from left to right. When it reaches the right of the box, it then begins again from the left.

Rule 2: The number of diagonal lines in the rectangle increases by one each time.

Rule 3: The orientation of the diagonal lines alternates each time.

Q15 What comes next in the sequence?

Answer = C

Rule 1: The symbol rotates 90° clockwise each time.

Rule 2: The black boxes move clockwise to the next corner each time.

Rule 3: The number of black boxes increases by one each time.

Q16 What comes next in the sequence?

Answer = B

Rule 1: The arrow rotates 45° counterclockwise each time.

Rule 2: The missing segment on the outer hexagon moves one place counterclockwise, then two places, then three and so on.

Rule 3: The inner hexagon alternates between black and white.

Q17 **What comes next in the sequence?**

Answer = D

Rule 1: The anchor rotates 135° counterclockwise each time.

Rule 2: The two main shaded halves of the anchor alternate between black and white.

Rule 3: The circle at the top of the anchor alternates between black and white.

Q18 **What comes next in the sequence?**

Answer = A

Rule 1: The triangle moves from top left, to bottom right, to bottom left, to top right and then begins again.

Rule 2: The square moves 5 places clockwise around the edge of the box (including centre and corner positions).

Rule 3: The circle moves down one place each time, beginning again at the top of the box.

Q19 **What comes next in the sequence?**

Answer = D

Rule 1: The boomerang moves from top left, to middle right, to bottom left, then begins again.

Rule 2: The boomerang rotates 90° clockwise each time.

Rule 3: The triangles on the boomerang alternate between black and white.

Q20 **What comes next in the sequence?**

Answer = E

Rule 1: The lines' orientation alternates between horizontal and vertical.

Rule 2: The total number of lines increases by two each time.

Rule 3: Every line is dashed, then every second line is dashed, then every third line is dashed and so on.

Q21 What comes next in the sequence?

Answer = B

Rule 1: The central square with the triangles alternates between black and white shading.

Rule 2: The unshaded circle moves two places clockwise each time.

Rule 3: The unshaded square moves three places clockwise each time.

Q22 What comes next in the sequence?

Answer = C

Rule 1: One line rotates 90° clockwise each time.

Rule 2: The other line 45° counterclockwise each time.

Rule 3: The black square moves one place clockwise each time.

Q23 What comes next in the sequence?

Answer = E

Rule 1: The number of edges on the outer shape decreases by one each time.

Rule 2: The number of edges on the inner shape increases by one each time.

Rule 3: The shapes alternate between black and white.

Q24 What comes next in the sequence?

Answer = D

Rule 1: The number of segments in the circle increases by one each time.

Rule 2: The arrow points to where the next arrow will be.

Rule 3: There are always 3 segments shaded.

Q25 **What comes next in the sequence?**

Answer = A

Rule 1: The white square moves down one place each time. When it reaches the bottom, it begins again from the top.

Rule 2: The first box is missing 1 square, the second box is missing 2 squares, the third box is missing 3 squares and so on.

Rule 3: The column with the missing squares moves one place to the right each time.

Q26 **What comes next in the sequence?**

Answer = E

Rule 1: The face goes from happy, to straight, to sad, to straight then happy and begins again.

Rule 2: The total number of freckles increases by one each time.

Rule 3: The eyes follow the black circle.

Q27 **What comes next in the sequence?**

Answer = C

Rule 1: The stripes on the lighthouse alternate between black and white.

Rule 2: The direction of the light coming from the lighthouse alternates between left and right.

Rule 3: The total number of stars in each box alternates between four and five.

Q28 **What comes next in the sequence?**

Answer = C

Rule 1: The box rotates 90° clockwise each time.

Rule 2: The total number of bricks in a box is the equal to the sum of bricks in the previous two boxes.

Rule 3: The number of shaded bricks increases by three each time.

Q29 What comes next in the sequence?

Answer = D

Rule 1: The shield rotates 45° counterclockwise each time.

Rule 2: The star moves two places clockwise each time.

Rule 3: The circle moves one place clockwise each time.

Q30 What comes next in the sequence?

Answer = A

Rule 1: The dividing line between black and white rotates 45° counterclockwise each time.

Rule 2: The two halves of the box alternate between black and white.

Rule 3: The circle moves back and forth along the dividing line, with each half again, alternating between black and white.

Chapter 9 Situational judgement tests

The brilliant learning from Chapter 9 was that you would understand what the questions in situational judgement tests are asking you to do and you would *have a clear strategy to minimise your stress and maximise your performance*. Here are the worked answers:

Scenario 1:

Situation 1

Responses:

(A) Prepare a presentation based on a detailed analysis of previous children's books on this topic that have done well and how they were promoted.

(This is the **least effective response** as this has no resemblance to the brief you were given. Also other members of the team may have been asked to look at the marketplace and competition for the client's products anyway. And finally, the client may be looking to see that you and your team can understand the uniqueness of their product rather than comparing it favourably or unfavourably to competitors' products.)

(B)   Prepare a presentation based on your experiences of learning about the environment as a child and your favourite books on the topic.

(**Not a particularly appropriate response** as you are not focusing on your client's products at all; you are presenting a 'personal' view, which may be of interest, but falling to talk about the most important thing, which is the product that you are pitching to promote.)

(C)   Prepare a presentation about how you felt and what questions came into your mind when you read the client's books.

(This is **the most effective response** as this is the brief you have been given by your team manager which is to give a personal and thoughtful view of the products; remember you are only one member of the team and therefore this will be your unique contribution whereas other team members will be able to talk about PR strategy, competition in the marketplace and to draw on more 'objective' analysis.)

(D)   Read the books to your nieces and nephews and prepare a presentation based on their response to the books.

(This is **a reasonable response** as you are presenting the views of a sample of the core market for the books: however, as the client has probably done work like this when developing the book series they may be less interested in this than they are in your views on the books. After all, you may be part of the team who eventually provide PR for the product. They will want to know that you like, and believe in, their books).

Situation 2

Responses:

(A) Delay the end of this project for as long as you can.

(This is **the least effective** response as you are affecting operational matters in the agency simply because of your own personal scheduling issues.)

(B) Ask your current team leader if she can assign some additional tasks to you to continue this placement a little longer.

(**A reasonable response** as you are already familiar with the market research department and will be able to contribute effectively to the team. It also buys you time with regard to seeking out your next placement or project.).

(C) Do nothing, as you will be able to use the 'downtime' after this project ends to pursue some personal development without having to work on a project for a while.

(**Not a particularly appropriate response** as you have not investigated why your next project hasn't come through – it may have been a simple oversight. You are supposed to be developing your skills 'on-the-job' and therefore you should be trying to secure new objectives and a new project on which to work.)

(D) Email your mentor to remind him that you think you are due to move on to a new posting or project in three days' time.

(This is **the most effective** response as a gentle reminder may facilitate the process. Or there may be reasons why you haven't been found a placement to move to and this way you will find out what they are and be able to act upon them).

Situation 3

Responses:

(A) Write a script for a telephone interview which your researchers will conduct with a sample of West Grimsdale households.

(**Not a particularly appropriate response** as, whilst this will need to be done at some point, it is not the most urgent element of the planning process. You can't write the script until you have clarified with the client exactly what they want to find out and whether there is more information that they would like gathered during the process.)

(B)   Find out how many households there are in West Grimsdale and into what social categories they fall.

(**A reasonable response**, as these are essential pieces of information required to help you plan your research and pick your sample of households to call. You clearly cannot call every household and will therefore need to select a representative sample from which you can draw conclusions about the whole of the WG region.)

(C)   Book some telephone researchers for three days next week to call households in West Grimsdale.

(This is **the least effective response** as you need to decide on your research approach before you book researchers otherwise you may book too few or too many and you may not be ready to start on the interview stage by next week anyway.)

(D)   Ask your team leader if you can have a meeting with the key contact at WGFRS in order to gain clarification on the detailed objectives of the research.

(This is **the most effective response** as you will need a detailed briefing from the client in order to be absolutely sure that you deliver what they want: they may have secondary information that they would like gathering at the same time as the information about the smoke-alarm fitting behaviour. Market research is expensive so the client will not want to waste an opportunity. Also, during the meeting you should be able to gather other information, such as local population demographics, which will help with your planning process).

Situation 4

Responses:

(A) Call Mr Jones immediately and apologise that he is unhappy. Ask exactly how you can improve the delivery of the project.

(This is **the most effective response** as you are acting swiftly to reduce Mr Jones's feelings of dissatisfaction and showing that you personally want to ensure his requirements are met).

(B) Email back and say that you have delivered all aspects of the project as agreed and attach a copy of the original project plan as proof.

(**Not a particularly appropriate response** as, whilst this may be true, you are not dealing with Mr Jones's views of the project. or indeed his feelings about how WGFRS have been treated.)

(C) Call Mr Jones' diary secretary and ask for a face-to-face meeting to be booked in to clear up the issues raised.

(**A reasonable response**, as a face-to-face meeting is always better than email or telephone for building relationships. However it may be even better to give an immediate (and apologetic) response to clear the air before having a meeting.)

(D) Inform your team leader that Mr Jones is being difficult and over-critical so she won't be surprised if she hears from him later.

(This is **the least effective response** as you are failing to respond to Mr Jones very quickly and this will do little to improve your working relationship with him; it is quite a defensive response.)

Scenario 2:

Situation 1

Responses:

(A) Be honest with Greta about your wishes and why you feel that it is important to you that you gain some experience on location. Ask her for her view on this and ask her whether there is any

chance that you can spend some time on the East Sussex shoot
before returning to the office to start your archiving project.

(The **second most effective response**. You are being upfront and
honest with Greta and asking for her view on your dilemma rather
than making demands directly. You are also making a reasonable
suggestion to which, hopefully, she will give fair consideration.)

(B)   Say you'd rather go to the location shoot in East Sussex as it
would support your development more than doing the archiving.

(The **least effective response**. This is, perhaps, too direct an
approach to take with a senior manager. It would be better to ask
Greta to participate in planning your development rather than
taking such a demanding tone with her.)

(C)   Agree to do the archiving project and ask Greta for a chance
today to talk about your learning and development, specifically
when you might get to do some location filming.

(The **most effective response**. Although you are missing out on
the location filming opportunity right now you are at least aiming
to get a development plan in place, one on which you and Greta
have agreed. If you include 'experiencing location filming' in your
development plan then Greta should give you an opportunity to
do this when the next chance arises. She may even allow you to
join the East Sussex shoot in its final week, if you are lucky).

(D)   Agree to do the archiving project – hopefully another chance to
experience location filming will arise soon.

(The **third most effective response**. Although you are keeping
Greta happy, she is still unaware of your aims and requirements.
After all, you are there 'to learn' in your role as an intern and
you are not managing your learning very well if you don't pursue
ways of filling the gaps in your experience. If you share your
objectives with Greta she will have the opportunity to help you
and support you.)

Situation 2

Responses:

(A) Cancel your attendance at the champagne preview event as you can always view the Battle of Hastings documentary another day in the office when you have more time.

(The **second most effective response**. It is correct to say that the preview event is the lowest priority of the two. However, it might be better to free up more time today rather than on Wednesday which is quite close to your deadline; it is probably wiser to drop both events as neither are essential activities.)

(B) Cancel your attendance at the media networking event tonight.

(The **third most effective response**. It is a good idea to give yourself extra time today to get a 'good run' at the task. However, you should perhaps drop both events as neither are essential activities and, given that the previous scout took a week to find appropriate locations, you will probably need all the time you can get and should be willing to re-prioritise less important – if enjoyable – events.)

(C) Call the relevant people and apologise that you won't be able to attend the evening events and say they should give your place to anyone who may be waiting for a ticket.

(The **most effective response** – given that the previous scout found three similar locations in a week and say you have only three days, all the time that you can find will probably be needed.

Also, you need to be willing to de-prioritise less' core' activities when deadlines are tight.)

(D) Tell Greta that you have two evening events planned before Thursday and that given the likely time it will take to find a relevant location perhaps she should assign another person to work alongside you on the task as well.

(The **least effective response**. This would be a reasonable approach to take if the evening events were high priority, however they are probably not and therefore you perhaps should be pre-pared to drop at least one of them in order to maximise your time available to pursue the location-scouting objective.)

Situation 3

Responses:

(A) Research the popularity of the three topics on the internet: looking at 'trending' topics on Twitter, fan sites and other information.

(The **second most effective response**. As long as you can analyse and evaluate the validity of the information well then this should give you a good insight into what will play well and is a low cost way of making the decision.)

(B) Give your recommendation based on which one most appeals to you as you are not that knowledgeable about art and therefore feel that you are an average viewer in that sense.

(The **least effective response**. This is essentially 'gut feel' and is not a sufficient factor on which to base such an important decision.)

(C) Do an online survey of people aged 14 to 25 and ask them which of the titles most appeals to them; recommend the title that is given the most votes.

(The **most effective response**. This is a reasonable approach with the caveat that your survey group must be big enough, that it represents a cross-section of locations across the UK and that the difference in number of votes between the three options should be significantly large – i.e. not just one or two votes either way.).

(D) Look at the viewing figures for previous documentaries on terrestrial TV which had similar topics.

(The **third most effective response**. This could be useful but the viewing figures alone don't tell you whether your target audience would be interested in the topics, only about the viewing public as a whole. You would need to be able to break down the audience data into age groups.) It may also be difficult to find close matches to your subject matter.).

Situation 4

Responses:

(A) Tell the professor that everyone gets nervous before filming and that you worked with a famous actor the other day who was suffering from performance anxiety just filming a 30-second trailer.

(The **third most effective response**. This may make the professor feel better, that even professional performers can get nervous; however he might need some more practical help as well.)

(B) Get the professor a cup of tea and let him sit down for a minute or two to collect himself.

(The **second most effective response**. Allowing him to relax and sit down for a while may help him be less anxious but you could give him some tips for how to tackle his nerves more actively.)

(C) Suggest that the professor takes deep breaths, relaxes his shoulders and imagines that he is in his lecture room back at university, not in a studio at all.

(The **most effective response**. You are giving the professor some practical, useful advice that might help him to deal with his nerves and the situation more effectively. You have to be careful that your advice is given respectfully as you are somewhat the 'junior' person in the situation.)

(D) Tell the professor that you're sure he'll be fine and not to worry.

(The **least effective response**. This is unlikely to convince the professor as you may not have that much credibility with him, being a relatively junior member of the team. Also, you are giving no advice, help or support to him at all.)

Scenario 3:

Situation 1

Responses:

(A) Apologise to the customer and say that unfortunately there is not much on Tradewinds' menu which will be appropriate for their diet but they could try the healthfood cafe on the High Street.

(This is the **least effective response** as you are not even attempting to serve the customer).

Note: this is a good example where you need to know the company you are applying to. Tailor your answers to their ethos. This response probably would be a good response for a large chain of coffee shops where customer volume is more important than friendly service.

(B) Say that your colleague would be happy to freshly prepare a salad without any cheese and ask if the customer would be happy to wait for a few moments whilst you find out about the soya latte. Ask your manager if you can pop out to the nearby convenience store for some soya milk to make the latte.

(This is the **most effective response** as you are making every effort possible, given the circumstances, to serve the customer something suitable. There is scope for you to leave the shop briefly as there should be two of your colleagues and the branch manager present in the shop at the present time).

Note: this response probably wouldn't go down well if the coffee shop was a large chain. This response is only effective in this scenario because we are told Tradewinds are focussed on customer service.

(C) Apologise for the lack of soya milk but offer to freshly prepare a salad without any dairy in it for the customer. Point out any other items in the shop that would be appropriate for their diet.

(**A reasonable response** but it's a shame not to have done everything you could to provide the soya milk alternative for the customer.)

(D) Suggest the customer go to the healthfood cafe on the High Street and, when the customer has gone, suggest to your manager that your branch introduce soya milk as an alternative for customers and make some non-dairy salads for vegans and people with restricted diets.

(**Not a particularly appropriate response** as, despite your good intentions for the future, this doesn't help the customer today who wanted to buy their lunch at Tradewinds.)

Situation 2

Responses:

(A) Say nothing, but try to hang back every now and then when customers come into the shop, giving Danielle the opportunity to serve a customer on her own.

(**Not a particularly appropriate response** as Danielle may be nervous or worried about serving customers because she isn't confident about some aspect of the process and you are forcing her into a situation where she may make mistakes.)

(B) Take the opportunity to talk to Danielle when there is a lull in service this morning. Ask if she is feeling OK about all aspects of the job and whether she would like you to review any processes or tasks with her to remind her what to do. Say that serving customers is probably the most important aspect of the job and it can also be the most rewarding as you get to meet and talk to all sorts of different people.

(This is **the most effective response** as you are offering Danielle support and an opportunity to ask for help if she needs it. You are also making the customer service aspect of the job seem appealing and hopefully this will encourage her to become more involved in doing this).

(C) Say to Danielle that you feel that the responsibility for serving customers is hers as well as yours. State that you don't think it's

▶

fair that you continue dealing with the vast majority of customers whilst she only does the paperwork and deliveries behind the scenes.

(This is **the least effective response** as Danielle is likely to feel that you are not a supportive colleague and so won't open up to you with regard to the reasons for her reluctance to serve customers. Also, you are not 'selling' the idea of serving customers to make it something attractive and exciting for Danielle.)

(D) When there is a chance this morning, ask Danielle if she would like to observe you serving a customer. Show her how enjoyable it can be to serve customers by chatting and being friendly to customers and letting her see how they respond.

(**A reasonable response** as it will hopefully enthuse Danielle about the customer service role. However you are offering little in the way of practical support to her in terms of skills review – for example, she may be worried about using the till.)

Situation 3

Responses:

(A) Start cashing up at 7.20pm in order to make sure that you have the full half-hour to spend on the cleaning.

(**Not a particularly appropriate response** as there may still be customers in the shop at 7.20pm and as you are alone on shift you would not be able to cash up securely.)

(B) Talk to your manager and ask for an extra 10 minutes' pay on the late shift so you can work until 8.10pm and finish the cleaning to the required standards.

(**A reasonable response**, although it may be better to see if you can achieve the work in the allowed time.)

(C) Work as fast as you can to complete the cleaning to the required standard and quickly do the cashing up.

(This is **the least effective response** as the cleaning has to be done thoroughly and to a high standard; rushing the job will have a possible negative impact on the quality of the work done.)

(D) Commence the cleaning and cashing up as usual at 7.30pm but tackle the jobs in a reasonable order of priority. You could leave the least hygiene-critical parts of the shop until last, for example the chairs, tables and floor in the customer area. As long as you have wiped these down you could leave a note for the morning shift saying that they need to give the area a more thorough clean first thing in the morning.

(This is **the most effective response** as, until the branch manager integrates the higher cleaning standard into the normal work routine, you are making sure that the safety-critical things are done properly within the allocated time.)

Situation 4

Responses:

(A) Ask the customer you are serving to excuse you for a minute. Turn to the pregnant woman and ask her if she is alright and whether she needs to sit down. If she says she does need to sit down then say that you or your colleague will come and take her order at her table so that she needn't stand any longer. Ask the young man behind her whether he is just buying cold food and drinks, in which case your colleague can serve him quickly after the second customer.

(This is **the most effective response** as, although you may not end up dealing with everyone strictly in order, you are dealing with each customer according to their needs and not leaving anyone feeling frustrated by the level of service).

(B) Finish serving your current customer as quickly as possible in order that the pregnant woman and impatient man don't have to wait too long.

(**Not a particularly appropriate response** as your current customer might feel dissatisfied with being rushed and the other customers still have to wait.)

(C) Tell the pregnant woman to take a seat at a table and your colleague or yourself will come and take her order soon.

(**A reasonable response,** however the woman may be feeling OK and you are making an assumption about her needs without checking first. Also the impatient man, and other customers in the queue, may feel put out that she is getting special treatment without it being obvious why.)

(D) Ask your colleague to keep serving at the till and go along the line of customers asking each one what their requirements are with regard to hot or cold food and drinks. Ask all those who only require cold food or drink to form a separate queue and serve these people quickly. Ask the other people to take a seat and wait for you to come and serve them in a minute.

(This is **the least effective response** as you are completely changing the serving system and without proper planning this could be chaotic. Also, you are not responding to the individual needs of the customers, just making the situation slightly more ordered for you and your colleague.)

Scenario 4:

Situation 1

Responses:

(A) Send an email to the ADF and the two councillors before the meeting giving a reasoned and evidence-based argument for why the budget cut is not appropriate. Prepare this argument in a bullet-point sheet for you to refer to in the meeting. Include points about voter and visitor reactions to the urban landscape.

(The **very effective** response. You are using evidence and logic to build a convincing argument against the cut, implying that visitor numbers may drop if the urban landscape is not as pretty, but also preparing your senior colleagues for what you are going to say so that they don't feel defensive in the meeting.)

(B) Send a copy of 'Encouraging Wildlife in Inner Cities' to each of the people with whom you will be meeting. It is a pamphlet that explains how roadside planting can encourage bats, birds and insects to thrive in the urban environment.

(The **ineffective** response. This is only one possible point to make about the benefits of planting and you are not taking the trouble to explain it in a brief format yourself.)

(C) Call the Director of Finance and ask him to attend the meeting as you want to talk to the person with 'the final say'.

(The **counterproductive** response. This is inappropriate because you are being rude and dismissive to the ADF and the councillors; also you are doing nothing to prepare a convincing case.)

(D) Ask for information from the LoSCC Countryside & Wildlife Officer with regard to the impact that planting schemes have had on wildlife. Prepare a document outlining this information to take to the meeting.

(The **slightly effective** response. You are preparing a reasoned argument, however it is a narrow one with no economic or political considerations which would be more likely to sway the ADF and the elected councillors.)

(E) Collate data on responses to the planting schemes from visitors and residents. Prepare an 'easy-to-digest' handout, for the ADF and the councillors, which outlines the key arguments for keeping the budget as it is. Hand copies of these out at the meeting.

(The **effective** response. You are using a sound, evidence-based argument but it would be even better to share this with your colleagues before the meeting in order that they have time to digest it and prevent them reacting defensively at the meeting.)

Situation 2

Responses:

(A) Split the paper into manageable chunks and prioritise these sections. Make sure that you and your colleague complete the high priority sections first and leave appendices, etc. until last. At least that way you can submit appendices and supplementary information later if they aren't complete by 4pm.

(The **effective** response. This is a logical approach and should mean that the key information relating to why the parking scheme is required will be presented and submitted on time.)

(B) Start writing the proposal immediately; work as hard as you can to get the entire paper written by 4pm.

(The **ineffective** response. You have no prioritisation of sections of the paper and you haven't agreed with your colleague who is doing what; this could lead to duplication and misdirected effort.)

(C) Ask your project manager to consider submitting the proposal to next month's committee meeting.

(The **counterproductive** response. Your PM requires the proposal to go through this month and delaying the submission would delay the whole project by four weeks or more.)

(D) Prioritise the sections of the report and share the high priority ones between the two of you, leaving the less important appendices until last. Also email the committee convener to see if there is any flexibility in the deadline.

(The **very effective** response. You are approaching the problem from two angles here by pushing back on the deadline but also assuming that, if it doesn't change, you should be able to produce something reasonable for submission on time.)

(E) Ask your PM to check why the submission has to be done by 4pm today (you assume that no one will be reading it overnight); ask for an extension to 9am tomorrow if at all possible.

(The **slightly effective** response. It is reasonable to question the deadline as the committee date has changed and there may be no actual need to complete the submission at 4pm. Although if the deadline is immovable then you will need a different approach.)

Situation 3

Responses:

(A) Consult a range of sources (including other local authorities, waste management industry experts, expert websites and previous LoSCC bid processes) and collate a longlist of possible criteria to present to your PM for discussion.

(The **very effective** response. By thoroughly researching the issue you will be bringing the 'best practice' ideas from outside LoSCC to the attention of your team.)

(B) Brainstorm ideas yourself 'from first principles'.

(The **ineffective** response. By doing this you risk generating only a very limited and narrow range of ideas.)

(C) Ask Wastewarriors to suggest a list of additional selection criteria.

(The **counterproductive** response. They will skew the criteria in their favour.)

(D) Ask for a meeting or phone call with the LoSCC Head of Waste Management and pick their brains as to what criteria might be appropriate.

(The **slightly effective** response. Some relevant suggestions will come from this, however the range of suggestions may be too narrow, you aren't introducing new ideas to LoSCC and the input of this manager is likely to be sought anyway. Therefore it is duplication of effort.)

(E) Gather a few other team members together for a brainstorming session to generate as many possible criteria as you can. Check this list against the expert information on the internet to provide a realistic list for presentation to your PM.

(The **effective** response. You may get some interesting, 'blue sky' ideas in this way although you may lose the benefit of spending the time doing wider research into 'tried and tested', approaches.)

Situation 4

Responses:

(A) Arrange a time next week for a sit down/lunch with Graham to talk through his problems in detail. Let him get all his problems 'off his chest' and then help him start to generate solutions to his time management challenges and ways that he can increase his personal resilience.

(The **effective** response. This could be very helpful for Graham; however it could be even more useful to introduce some 'best practice' ideas from elsewhere, not just the solutions that the two of you can come up with.)

(B) Take him out for a drink and help him forget about his troubles and unwind for at least one night.

(The **ineffective** response. You are doing nothing constructive to help Graham tackle his problems.)

(C) Feel relieved that there will be one less person to compete with for LoSCC management jobs and wish him luck in the future.

(The **counterproductive** response. You are being unsupportive towards Graham, unhelpful to your employer – as graduates cost money to develop and train and this money will be wasted – and also, you will lose a colleague who could be helpful and supportive of you in the future.)

(D) Suggest Graham talks his problems through with his graduate mentor.

(The **slightly effective** response. Graham will benefit from a talk with someone qualified to deal with these kinds of issues; however he may feel more comfortable chatting things through first with a peer such as you.)

(E) Suggest a time next week when you will be available for a longer chat with Graham. Bring along some time management/stress management books to show Graham. Listen to his problems in detail.

(The **very effective** response. Graham may benefit greatly from a friendly, listening ear. You can use the books as inspiration for possible approaches Graham could take to tackle his problems. Following this session Graham may feel more confident in approaching his mentor and confiding in her as well.)

Chapter 10 Personality tests

The brilliant learning from Chapter 10 was that you would understand what personality tests are asking you to do and that you would have a clear strategy about tackling them. If you registered on the Assessment Day website when you took their online personality test, you will have received feedback online. (www.assessmentday.co.uk/)

Online practice

There are plenty of online sites where you can practise psychometric tests; this is just a selection. Take a look at the organisation/employer you are applying for; they will often have practice tests on their own site, or signpost where the tests they use are offered for practice.

Assessment Day   www.assessmentday.co.uk/

All the practice tests included in this text are from Assessment Day (with their kind permission). Their site offers a great deal both in terms of what you can access without charge as well as what you can purchase. With the free practice questions, you get an instant snapshot of your scores, including useful detail, such as number of questions attempted, number of questions correctly answered, time taken and percentile score. You can even upload your practice test results onto your Facebook wall (if you really want to).

The site also gives links to employers' own practice SJTs, because commissioning bespoke tests is more common. Being aware of the company value-set will help in checking if you are going to feel right for the company you're applying for.

Cubiks   www.cubiksonline.com/cubiks/practicetests

This is a neat and tidy site which is easy to find your way around. It is helpful in giving tips on how to go about tests, and a there's a useful intervention which tells you immediately you've got an answer wrong and prompts you to have another go. However, it doesn't really explain exactly how to tackle a question and work through it to the correct answer. The candidate area of the site does include practice questions and there is a diagrammatic reasoning leaflet which provides a helpful explanation. The free offer includes only two example questions.

Saville and Holdsworth   www.shldirect.com/en

This is a long established test publisher. The website covers the full range of assessment methods and recruitment practice, explaining why employers opt for this approach and how they use the assessment toolkit. There is good, practical advice to candidates on how to prepare before tests and how to behave during an assessment centre, and the site also provides fast links to practice sites, which are comprehensive. Example questions are given (typically two for each kind of test) and these allow a second attempt if incorrect on first go. They give a clear indication of how to work out the correct answer – that is, how to set about answering the question. Many of the tests require payment but some of the online trial tests offer the chance to enter a prize draw.

This site also has a commendably clear section on Disabled Talent which shows the kind of additional support which can be put in place where candidates have particular needs.

Talentlens   www.talentlens.co.uk

This showcases what Pearson offers to talent management, particularly through the use of psychometrics. It is a comprehensive offering, ranging across levels beyond (but including) graduates. It has useful information on what tests do and lots of technical information. There are some sample questions and, particularly where a new instrument is in development, valuable opportunities to take an entire, timed test on-line. The blogs are really interesting, not only about testing but about development both for individuals and organisations.

TalentQ   www.trytalentq.com/

TalentQ has a comprehensive online site, which includes all the reasoning, situational judgement and personality tests. They provide some free online practice tests and plenty of tips on what tests do and how to prepare for them. A distinguishing feature of their online testing is their adaptive approach, which offers a customised testing experience by taking into account the way you answered a question before presenting you with the next question. So if your first answer was both swift and accurate, the next question would be selected to stretch you further.

Bibliography

British Psychological Society (BPS) (2012) *Psychological Testing: A Test-Taker's Guide*. BPS Steering Committee on Test Standards. online: **http://psychtesting.org.uk**

British Psychological Society (undated) *Psychological terms.* online: **www.bps.org.uk/psychology-public/psychological-terms/ psychological-terms**

Civil Service (2013) *What is Fast Stream Assessment Centre?*

International Test Commission (2010) *A Test-Taker's Guide to Technology-Based Testing.* online: **www.intestcom.org**

What did you think of this book?

We're really keen to hear from you about this book, so that we can make our publishing even better.

Please log on to the following website and leave us your feedback.

It will only take a few minutes and your thoughts are invaluable to us.

www.pearsoned.co.uk/bookfeedback

Index